A DICTIONARY FOR CATHOLICS

LAURIE WOODS

 HarperCollins*Religious*
An imprint of HarperCollins*Publishers*

HarperCollins*Religious*
An imprint of HarperCollins*Publishers*, Australia

First published in Australia in 1990
Revised edition published in 1999 by HarperCollins*Religious*
ACN 008 431 730
A member of HarperCollins*Publishers* (Australia) Pty Limited
Level 3/150 Jolimont Road,
East Melbourne, Victoria 3002, Australia
http://www.harpercollinsreligious.com.au

HarperCollins*Publishers*
25 Ryde Road, Pymble, Sydney NSW 2073, Australia
31 View Road, Glenfield, Auckland 10, New Zealand
75-85 Fulham Palace Road, London W6 8JB, United Kingdom
Hazelton Lanes, 55 Avenue Road, Suite 2900, Toronto, Ontario, M5R 3L2
and 1995 Markham Road, Scarborough, Ontario M1B 5M8, Canada
10 East 53rd Street, New York NY 10022, USA

The National Library in Australia Cataloguing-in-Publication data:

Woods, Laurie.
    Dictionary for Catholics
    ISBN 1 86371 781 1.
    1. Catholic Church – Dictionaries, Juvenile. I. Title.
282.03

Nihil Obstat: Reverend Gerard Diamond MA (Oxon), LSS, D. Theol
                 Diocesan Censor

Imprimatur: Most Reverend Denis J Hart DD
               Vicar General

Date: 30 August 1999

The Nihil Obstat and Imprimatur are official declarations that a book or pamphlet is free of doctrinal
or moral error. No implication is contained therein that those who have granted the Nihil Obstat
and Imprimatur agree with the contents, opinions or statements expressed. They do not necessarily signify
that the work is approved as a basic text for catechetical instruction.

Illustrations by John Nicholson

Printed in China by RR Donnelley
on 120gsm Woodfree

Contents

Contributors and Consultants

This revised edition edited by Laurie Woods.

Project Director (1990): Dr Anne Benjamin

Edited (1990) by: Laurie Woods, with contributions from
                          Fr Ross Naylor, Mr Geoff Plant,
                          Mrs Pat Reiher, Mr Gerard Sullivan,
                          Dr Kevin Treston.

Consultants (1990):   Graham Barry, Fr Paul Crowley,
                          Graham English, Dr Charles Hill,
                          Philippa Merchant, Michael Murray,
                          Sr Margaret Press, Fr Joseph Takchi,
                          Kay Taylor, Peter Vyverberg.

Abba (Aramaic form of *ab*, father.) This term is used by Jewish children in a loving way. It corresponds to our word 'dad'. Jesus used this word when he prayed to his heavenly Father (Mark 14:36).

Abbess Leader of a community of nuns who take vows of poverty, chastity and obedience and live together in a house or a building called a convent.

Abbot (Aramaic *abba*, father.) Leader of a community of men, called monks, who live in a monastery. The abbot is normally elected by the monks of the monastery.

Ablutions (Latin *ablutio*, washing.) A ceremony of washing. In the liturgy the priest washes his fingers at the preparation of the gifts and he washes the sacred vessels after communion.

Absolution (Latin *absolutio*, forgiveness.) An action where the priest passes on God's forgiveness to a person in the sacrament of Reconciliation.

Abstinence, day of (Latin *abstinere,* keep away from something.) A day when people should not eat meat. Ash Wednesday and Good Friday are days of abstinence. On Ash Wednesday, as a sign of repentance, Catholics should not eat meat. On Good Friday, as a sign of mourning for the death of Christ, they should not eat meat. Abstinence is also an act of self-control that will help Christians gain strength of spirit.

ACC *See* Australian Council of Churches.

Acclamation (Latin *acclamare*, shout, applaud.) Words or songs of announcement, approval or applause. In the liturgy there are times when the people answer 'Amen' or 'Thanks be to God'. These are acclamations. The short verse that is sung or recited before the gospel at Mass announces the reading. This is called the gospel acclamation.

Acolyte (Greek *akolouthos*, attendant.) A person who assists the priest or deacon in the celebration of the liturgy. Acolytes distribute Holy Communion at Mass and also Communion to the sick.

ACR *See* Australian Catholic Relief.

Act of Contrition (Latin *contritus,* wiped way, upset.) A prayer in which we say we are truly sorry for our sins.

Acts Short reference to the *Acts of the Apostles*, the book that is a sequel to the Gospel of Luke. It was written about fifty years after the death of Jesus, and tells the story of the people who brought the 'Good News' from Jerusalem to Rome and the wider world. The chief characters of the Acts are St Peter and St Paul.

Acts of Martyrs Collection of stories about the early Christian martyrs. Some stories are authentic, but some have been changed.

Adam (Hebrew *adamah*, earth.) The name given to the character who represents all human beings in the stories of Genesis 1–4.

Adonai Hebrew word meaning 'the Lord'. It was one of the ways of referring to God in the Hebrew scriptures.

Adoration (Latin *adorare*, to speak to, worship.) The offering of worship to God.

Adoration of the Most Blessed Sacrament An act of worship given to Jesus in the sacrament of the Eucharist. Sometimes the host may be put in a special container (*see* Monstrance) on the altar so that worshippers may see it.

Advent (Latin *adventus*, an approach, arrival.) A period of prayer in preparation for the coming of Christ at Christmas. There are four Sundays in Advent, which begins the Church's liturgical year.

Advocate One who speaks in defence of, or on behalf of, somebody else. The Holy Spirit helps Christians and acts in their defence and is therefore called the Advocate. *See also* Paraclete.

Agape A Greek word meaning 'love'. It was the name given to the eucharistic meal or love feast at which the early Christians remembered the Lord Jesus.

Agnostic A person who is convinced that we cannot know whether or not there is a God.

Agnus Dei Latin words meaning the 'Lamb of God'. (1) A prayer to Jesus recited or sung in the Mass before Communion. *See* Lamb of God. (2) The picture of a lamb, which represents Jesus Christ holding a victory banner with a red cross on it.

Aisle (1) That part of a church that forms the wings on either side of the centre or nave. (2) The walkways between the pews or seats of a church.

Alb (Latin *albus*, white.) A long, white garment worn by ministers of the Eucharist. It is worn by bishops and priests underneath the other vestments at Mass.

Alexandria The second largest city of the Roman Empire, situated near the Nile delta in northern Egypt. Alexandria had a large Jewish community in the first century before the coming of Christ. It became an important centre for learning during the second and third centuries CE.

All Saints A feast day celebrated on 1 November to honour all those saints or holy people who have gone before us into heaven. In a particular way the Church honours those good and holy people who do not have a special feast day celebrated during the year.

All Souls 2 November. A special day of prayer and remembrance for all those who have died.

Alleluia Hebrew word meaning 'praise the Lord'. It was used mostly at times of prayer and worship in the Temple. The priest would cry 'hallelu' (praise!), and the people would shout the first part of God's name, Yahweh. It would sound like 'hallelu – Ya!'.

Alpha and Omega The first and last letters of the Greek alphabet. They stand for God, who is the beginning and the end of all things. The symbol also represents Jesus (Revelation 22:13).

Altar Usually a stone table or structure on which sacrifices were offered to gods in former times. The people of ancient Israel built altars on which to offer fruit and animal sacrifices. Their chief altar was in the Temple in Jerusalem. In the Catholic Church the altar is the Lord's table at which the people of God celebrate the Eucharist. Christians have traditionally called the Eucharist a sacrifice because it commemorates the fact that Jesus gave himself up for everyone, so the altar is the table at which Christ's sacrifice of himself on the cross is remembered and made present.

Altar bread Wafers of bread baked without yeast and used as hosts for Communion in the Roman rite.

Altar cloth A cloth of linen that covers the altar.

Altar of repose A temporary altar, in which the Blessed Sacrament is kept from Holy Thursday evening until Holy Saturday night.

Altar stone A flat piece of stone containing the relics of a martyr. It fits into a specially made slot on the top of a consecrated altar. If the altar has not been consecrated the altar stone is not required.

Ambo (Greek *ambon*, raised place.) A raised platform with steps leading up to it. It was near the altar, and the scriptures were read from it. Today it refers to the reading stand (lectern) from which the lector reads the scripture at Mass.

Amen Hebrew word meaning 'certainty', 'it is true'. The word 'Amen' is commonly found at the end of prayers. When a group of people say 'Amen' at the end of a prayer it shows they agree with the thoughts and feelings expressed in the prayer.

Amice (Latin *amicire*, to wrap around.) The first vestment put on by a priest in vesting for Mass. It is an oblong linen cloth worn across the shoulders underneath the alb. The wearing of the amice is optional.

Anabaptists A Christian group in the sixteenth century who refused to allow their children to be baptised. They taught that baptism should be only for adult believers of the Christian faith.

Anamnesis A Greek word meaning 'memorial', 'calling to mind'. It is that part of the Eucharistic Prayer which begins just after the acclamation that follows the consecration. The anamnesis recalls Jesus Christ's work of redemption through his life, death, resurrection and ascension.

Anaphora (Greek *anaphorein*, offer up.) A name for the Eucharistic Prayer, which begins with the Preface and ends with the Great Amen just before the Our Father.

Angel (Greek *angelos*, messenger.) Angels are spirit beings sent as messengers from God to humans or Satan. For instance, the angel Gabriel gave a message to Mary the mother of Jesus (Luke 1:26ff.); in the book of Tobit, the angel Raphael appeared to Tobit and acted as his guide.

Angelus A prayer said with three 'Hail Marys' and sayings from the scripture, taken from the story of the Annunciation, to commemorate the coming of Jesus into the world. It is intended to be recited three times a day at the ringing of the Angelus bells. The prayer has its origins in the Middle Ages.

Anglican Name given to those Christians baptised into the Church of England. The Anglican Church was founded after a break with the Roman Church in the sixteenth century, and soon became the dominant church in England. In Australia this Church is known as the Anglican Church in Australia.

Anno Domini (AD) Latin, 'in the year the Lord'—that is, the year of Our Lord's birth. Our dates are set from the birth of Christ. AD is now being replaced by CE (Common Era), which is more acceptable to those people who do not believe in the importance of Jesus Christ in the same way that Christians do.

Annulment A decision by a Church court saying that a particular marriage is not a true sacramental marriage in the eyes of the Church. Such a decision would be made when one or more of the conditions for a true sacramental marriage has not been fulfilled. For example, if one or both of the parties had been forced into the marriage, the condition of 'free consent' to the marriage would not have been fulfilled.

Annunciation An announcement or proclamation. It has a special meaning when it refers to the announcement made by the angel Gabriel to Mary that God had chosen her to be the mother of Jesus. The feast of the Annunciation of the Lord is 25 March.

Anointing of the Sick A sacrament in which a sick person is anointed with blessed olive oil by a bishop or priest. The oil, which is a sign of healing by the Holy Spirit, is usually put on the sick person's forehead and hands in the form of a cross. The sacrament is a sign of the love and care that God and the Church have for people who are sick.

Anthem A psalm or hymn sung during an act of worship.

Antioch The third-largest city in the Roman Empire, situated on the Orontes River in south-eastern Turkey. It was at Antioch that the followers of Jesus were first called 'Christians'.

Antiphon Lines or passages taken from scripture or other books and sung or recited in turns by parts of a choir or group. For example, the response in the responsorial psalm is an antiphon

Anti-Semitism (Latin *anti*, against; *Semite* from Shem the eldest son of Noah.) Hatred of Jewish people and their organisations.

Apocalypse (Greek *apokalypsis*, revelation.) The Apocalypse of John is a book describing the visions that the author had about the early Christians and the struggles they had with the pagan people around them. In this time of crisis the writer tried to give people courage and tell them to keep trusting in God. The Apocalypse is also called the Book of Revelation.

Apocalyptic Adjective from apocalypse, referring to any description of visions and dreams, particularly those dealing with the end of the world. These visions were described in highly imaginative language, using fantasy and symbolism.

Apocrypha (Greek *apokryphos*, hidden.) The apocrypha or apocryphal books are religious writings of the ancient Jews and Christians not included in the Bible. Certain books that are included in Catholic editions of the Old Testament are called apocryphal by Jews and Protestants.

Apologetics The branch of theology that tries to show that the Christian faith is reasonable, and can be defended against the arguments of those who attack it.

Apologists (Greek *apologia*, a speech in defence.) Christian writers in the early Church who defended the faith and wrote about their beliefs.

Apostasy (Greek *apostasia*, a turning away.) The act of giving up Christianity and going over to paganism. The early Christians regarded this as one of the worst sins.

Apostle (Greek *apostolos*, someone who is sent as a messenger or agent.) This refers especially to the twelve followers of Jesus who were sent out to preach the good news of salvation (Matthew 28:19; Luke 6:13; 9:10). St Paul is also called the Apostle to the Gentiles. *See also* Disciple.

Apostles' Creed A summary of Christian teaching named after the Apostles because it contains twelve statements of faith.

Apostolate The particular task or mission of a person who works for the spiritual good of others.

Apostolic Delegate A person (usually a bishop) who represents the Pope in a foreign country in official business with the bishops of that country.

Apostolic Fathers Leading Christian writers of the first and second centuries who passed on the teachings of the Apostles, e.g. St Clement of Rome, St Ignatius of Antioch.

Apparition (Latin *apparitio*, appearance.) A vision or unusual mystical appearance of some person or thing, usually with a message. For instance, it is believed by many that Jesus appeared to St Margaret Mary Alacoque; and that Mary appeared to St Bernadette at Lourdes, to the three children at Fatima; and more recently to the young people at Medjugorje in Yugoslavia. Catholics are not obliged to believe in the reality of apparitions such as these. The messages of these events are not equal to the Gospel itself.

Apse (Greek *hapsis*, loop, circle.) The semicircular end of old church buildings in which the altar is placed. The apse was always at the eastern end of the church.

Aramaic The language spoken in Palestine by Jews in New Testament times. It was the mother tongue of Jesus. It is closely related to Hebrew. *See also* Hebrew.

Archbishop (Greek *archos*, chief; *episkopos*, bishop.) A bishop who is in charge of an archdiocese.

Archimandrite (Greek *archos*, chief; *mandra,* monastery.) (1) The superior of one or more monasteries in the Eastern churches. (2) A title given to certain distinguished monks or unmarried priests.

ARCIC The Anglican-Roman Catholic International Commission set up by the Pope and the Archbishop of Canterbury in 1969. It is a group of clerical and lay scholars from the Roman Catholic and the Anglican churches who study and work for union and understanding between Catholics and Anglicans.

Arianism A heresy named after Arius, a priest of Alexandria in the fourth century, who taught that Jesus Christ was human but not divine. Because Arianism was so influential and widespread the Emperor Constantine called an ecumenical council at Nicea in 325 CE to combat it.

Ark A box or chest. Noah's Ark was the vessel that Noah built to preserve himself and his family and pairs of different animals from the flood (Genesis 6).

Ark of the Covenant A wooden box overlaid with gold inside and out, which contained the tablets of stone on which the law of Moses was inscribed (Exodus 25:10ff.). It represented the presence of God among the people. The Israelites carried the ark around with them during their wandering in the desert. It was taken by the Babylonian army in 586 BCE. Finally, it was housed in the Temple in Jerusalem, in a special room called the Holy of Holies.

Armenian Church Armenia, the country north-east of Turkey, has always been noted for its large number of devout Christians. The Church in Armenia was split in 451 CE, and while some followed the Roman Church, most Armenians formed a separate church. Today there are Armenian Catholics and Armenian Orthodox Christians.

Armenian rite The liturgy of the Church of Armenia, which is a combination of Syrian and Cappadocian elements based on the Greek Liturgy of St Basil. It is celebrated in the classical Armenian language and is used by both Catholic and Orthodox Armenians.

Ascension A holy day (forty days after Easter) which celebrates the mystery that Christ left his disciples and went to his Father. The story told in Acts 1:6–11 is a dramatic way of expressing the truth that Jesus is in his heavenly home in the presence of God, and is watching over his people on earth.

Ascetic (Greek *ascetes*, monk, hermit, originally an athlete.) A person inspired by the love of God who practises penance, prayer and self-control to an extraordinary degree.

Ash Monday The first day of Lent in the Eastern Churches.

Ash Wednesday The first day of the season of Lent in many Christian churches. At the liturgy of Ash Wednesday ashes are blessed and marked on the foreheads of the people in the form of a cross. This is a reminder that we have turned away from sin and are trying to live the Christian life well.

Asperges (Latin *aspergere*, sprinkle.) A ritual of blessing the people and sprinkling them with holy water to symbolise cleansing them of sin. It is one of the forms of the Penitential rite that can be used at the beginning of Mass.

Aspirations (Latin *aspirare*, breathe on.) Very short prayers which may be said in a breath. For example, 'Jesus have mercy on me'.

Assumption A holy day (15 August) which celebrates the mystery that the Virgin Mary was taken into heaven body and soul. This was declared a doctrine of faith by Pope Pius XII in 1950.

Atheist A person who does not believe that there is a God.

Atonement The act of healing the broken relationship between God and human beings. Through the life, death and resurrection of Jesus we have been made one with God.

Australian Catholic Relief An organisation set up by the Australian bishops in 1964 to (1) help people understand the needs of the poor in the world and (2) raise money in Australia to support people who work for justice and human development in Australia and overseas. The best-known appeal of ACR is Project Compassion.

Australian Council of Churches An ecumenical organisation with about twelve member churches that was set up in 1946 to work for the spread of the Christian faith and unity among Christian churches in Australia and to assist Third World churches.

Auxiliary bishop A bishop who, for various reasons, assists the bishop of a diocese in his work.

Babylon Capital city of Babylonia (present-day Iraq). The Babylonian people were under the power of the Assyrians until 612 BCE, when they began to conquer other countries. They destroyed Jerusalem in 587 BCE, and took the leading citizens back to Babylon as exiles. This period of exile lasted until around 539 BCE.

Baptism (Greek *baptizein*, to dip or push under water.) A ceremony in which the person being baptised is bathed in water, or has water poured over his/her head. It is a sign of death to sin and rising to new life. People who are being baptised are saying they believe in Jesus Christ and want to be Christians. When babies are baptised the parents and godparents speak for them. Baptism is the primary sacrament of initiation by which an adult or child is received into the Church, the community of faith, which is the body of Christ. At baptism the new Christian receives the Holy Spirit and forgiveness of all sin.

Baptism of the Lord John the Baptist performed a symbolic washing, or baptism, of people who came to him because they were sorry for their sins. This washing was a sign of cleansing. John the Baptist baptised Jesus in the River Jordan (Matthew 3:13–17).

Baptismal font (Latin *fons*, a spring of water.) A pool or container that holds the water for baptism. The earliest baptismal fonts were deep enough to allow those being baptised to walk down into the water. In modern times the baptismal font usually stands somewhere inside the church, and in most churches it is raised or mounted on a stand to make it easier for the priest to pour water on the head of the baby.

Baptismal promises Declarations made at the time of baptism of belief in Jesus Christ and the Church, and the intention to lead a good Christian life. When an infant is baptised the promises are made by the parent and godparents.

Baptistery (1) A small building, originally separate from the church, in which baptisms took place. (2) A space within a church, separate from the main hall of worship, for baptisms. In both cases there is a font in the baptistery. Most modern churches tend not to have baptisteries and baptisms are celebrated in the sanctuary.

Baptists A name for a variety of Protestant groups who stress the importance of adult baptism. The Baptist Church is organised by the decision of the members who worship under a pastor of their own choice.

Basilica A Latin word meaning a large rectangular building, like a hall with a roof. Christians built basilicas for worship from the fourth century onwards. Before that time they usually met in private houses to eat the Lord's Supper.

BCE Before the Common Era. This is often used as a replacement of BC (before Christ) when giving dates in ancient history.

Beatific vision Those who die in union with God enjoy the beatific vision, which means they see God face to face and are completely happy forever.

Baptismal font

Beatitude (Latin *beatus*, blessed, happy.) A phrase that begins 'Blessed are ...' (Matthew 5:2–12; Luke 6:20ff.). Praise of people who are good and loving in their lives. Matthew used the beautiful Greek word *makarios*, which is a happiness that has its secret within itself; it cannot be taken away. It knows that sometimes there are tears and sadness, but it is not crushed by them.

Beelzebub 'The Lord of the Flies'. This is a joke name used by the Israelites for the Philistine god, whose proper name is Beelzebul (prince of the earth). *See* Matthew 10:25 and 12:24.

Believer In the Catholic tradition a believer is a person who trusts in God as a personal, loving all-powerful Being and who has faith in the great mysteries of the Trinity and the Incarnation. A believer tries to live according to the teachings and values of Jesus and his Church.

Benediction A rite in which the people are blessed with the Blessed Sacrament. *See* Blessing.

Benedictus *See* Canticle of Zachary.

Bible (Greek *biblos*, papyrus, roll of papyrus, book). A collection of 72 sacred books. It is divided into two main sections: (1) the Hebrew scriptures or Old Testament, which contains books of history, prophecy, poetry, wise sayings, etc.; (2) the New Testament, which contains the gospels, Acts, the letters written by leading Christians, and the Apocalypse of John. *See also* Word of God.

Bible service A prayer service which consists of three parts: (1) the reading of God's word; (2) a homily or sermon on the readings; (3) responses from the people in song, silence or any other form of prayer.

Biblical languages Most of the Hebrew scriptures were written in Hebrew, although some later sections were written in Aramaic, and then translated into Greek in the second century BCE. Jesus himself spoke Aramaic, which is related to Hebrew. The New Testament was written in Greek.

Bidding prayer A prayer asking for favours for the living or dead. Prayers of the Faithful at Mass are examples of bidding prayers.

Bishop (Greek *episkopos*, supervisor.) A priest who is specially ordained to teach, lead and look after spiritual needs of a particular group of people, usually a diocese. In early Christian times the bishop was called an *episkopos* and his function was to take care of both the spiritual and material concerns of his people.

Blessed The title given to holy persons who have died and who are being considered for canonisation. Before such people are officially declared to be saints they are called 'blessed'.

Blessed Sacrament Name for the Eucharist in which Jesus Christ is really present. It is kept in the tabernacle of the church so that it can be taken to the sick and given to the people of God outside Mass time, e.g. during a communion service. A third reason for preserving the Blessed Sacrament is that the people may come and adore Jesus Christ and nourish a deep spiritual friendship with him. The full meaning of the Blessed Sacrament can only be appreciated in the action of the community eucharistic liturgy.

Blessing The act of asking God's favour on a person or thing. When God blesses us we receive favours such as forgiveness, life, strength and happiness.

Blessing of the holy oils A ceremony carried out during a special Mass on Holy Thursday morning in which the bishop blessed the oils used in the sacraments of Baptism, Anointing of the Sick, Confirmation and Orders.

Blood In the Hebrew scriptures it is equivalent to life. Blood was shed at the sacrifice of an animal, as a sign that the persons offering the victim wanted to offer themselves entirely to God. It was then sprinkled at the base of the altar and on the people. Jesus shed his blood on the cross as the sign of the new covenant between God and humanity. In the sacrament of the Eucharist Christians share in the new life of Jesus.

Body of Christ This term refers to (1) the human body of Jesus, (2) the sacrament of the real presence of Jesus Christ under the appearance of bread and wine, and (3) all Christians who are united with Christ through baptism and as one body when their minds and hearts are in harmony with Jesus Christ.

Breaking of bread A name for the Eucharist used by early Christians. It came from the Jewish custom of beginning a meal with a prayer of thanks and a praise to God spoken over a loaf of bread, which was then divided up among those at the table. Jesus began his Last Supper with this custom.

Breviary A book containing a shorter portable edition of the Divine Office. *See* Divine Office.

Brother (1) In the Hebrew scriptures relatives (e.g. cousins, nieces/nephews) and even members of the same tribe were referred to as brothers or sisters. (2) Male member of a religious community who takes vows of poverty, chastity and obedience and is not a priest.

Buddhism A religion that began in India in the sixth century BCE and is based on the teaching of Siddhartha Gautama, the Buddha (the Enlightened One). Buddha taught that suffering in life is caused by wanting things. Buddhists believe that when they are free from all desires they reach supreme peace and happiness which is called Nirvana. Through meditation and leading a good life a Buddhist moves closer to this state of Nirvana. Buddhism is widely spread in India, Tibet, China, Thailand, Sri Lanka and Japan. It has also become popular in many Western countries.

Byzantine rite The ceremonies and liturgical customs based on the rite of St James of Jerusalem and the churches of Antioch, and reformed by St Basil and St John Chrysostom. It properly belongs to the Church of Byzantium (now called Istanbul) and is used by most of the Eastern Catholic and Orthodox churches.

Calendar (Latin *calendae*, the first day of the Roman month.) A system for calculating and organising days, months and years. The calendar used in most Western countries today is the Gregorian calendar, which was drawn up in 1582 by Pope Gregory XIII. The Eastern Orthodox churches do not follow this calendar, but continue to follow the Julian calendar introduced by Julius Caesar in 46 BCE. Other groups, such as Muslims and Jews, have their own calendars, which differ from the Gregorian calendar.

Calvary (Latin *calvaria,* skull.) The place just outside the city of Jerusalem where Jesus was executed. Criminals were commonly executed there and so it was called 'the place of the skull'. *See also* Golgotha.

Calvinism The Christian movement founded by the French Protestant reformer John Calvin (1509–1564). Calvin taught that God became known through the visible world and the scriptures. He also taught that God was supremely powerful and had selected some people to be saved and others to be punished and damned for ever, and no one knew for sure who was selected. Calvin's form of Christianity was severe. The Presbyterian Church is based on the teachings of Calvin.

Canaan The ancient name of the land that the Israelites occupied and called Israel. Some think the name came from the purple dye used by the original people who were ruled over by King Og. The Canaanite people had a big influence on the religion, literature and general culture of the Israelites.

Candle Blessed candles made of beeswax and tallow were used by the early Christians in their liturgical ceremonies, which were held mostly on Saturday evening and early Sunday morning.

Candlemas Feast of the Presentation of Our Lord in the Temple, 2 February. It is called Candlemas because candles are blessed on that day.

Canon (Greek *kanon*, rule, measure.) The list of books that have been accepted by the Church's teaching authority as sacred because they are inspired by God. *See also* Inspiration. There are other books, the apocryphal books, which are not part of the canon of scripture because they were not officially accepted.

Canon Law The official collection of Church laws for the Roman Church. It was revised and updated in accordance with the teaching of the Second Vatican Council. The revised form was published in 1983. The Eastern Churches in communion with Rome also have their own code of Canon Law, which takes into account their special traditions, laws and customs.

Canonisation Official declaration by the Pope that a person who has lived a good life and is in heaven may be publicly honoured as a saint.

Canticle of Mary In Luke's Gospel, a song of praise to God sung by the mother of Jesus when she visited her cousin Elizabeth (Luke 1:46–55). This song is often called the Magnificat, because the first words in its Latin translation are *magnificat anima mea* 'my spirit gives praise' (to God). This canticle echoes the song of Hannah, the mother of the great Hebrew leader Samuel. Hannah praised God and prayed for the poor and lowly people (1 Samuel 2:1–10).

Canticle of Simeon In Luke's Gospel, a song sung by Simeon, the elderly prophet in the Temple who blessed the baby Jesus. Simeon knew that Jesus was to be the Messiah, and he thanked God for allowing him to be alive to see the baby Jesus. After that he was happy to die in peace. This canticle is also called the *Nunc dimittis* 'Now you can let your servant go' after the first words in the Latin version.

Canticle of Zachary In Luke's Gospel, a song sung by Zachary, the father of John the Baptist, on the occasion of John's naming day (Luke 1:68–79). Zachary praised God and prophesied that the Messiah was about to come, and that his son, John, would prepare the way for the great one. This song is also called the *Benedictus* 'Blessed be …' after the first word in the Latin version.

Cantor Chief singer and often director of a church choir.

Capuchins (Italian *cappuccio*, a hood.) A religious order of men named after the hood they wear. It is a branch of the Franciscan order.

Cardinal (Latin *cardo*, hinge.) Priest or bishop appointed to the highest-ranking Church office under the Pope. The Sacred College of Cardinals assists the Pope with important issues and is also responsible for electing the Pope.

Cardinal virtues Important qualities of a good character. The virtues of prudence, justice, temperance and fortitude are given the name cardinal because other virtues hinge on them. We get these virtues when we co-operate with God's grace.

Carmelites Religious orders of women and men who trace their beginnings back to groups of Christian hermits living on Mt Carmel in the time of the Crusades to the Holy Land. St Teresa of Avila and St John of the Cross were Carmelites who reformed the order.

Carol A joyful song about the birth of Jesus at Christmas.

Cassock An ankle-length gown worn by clerics, usually of black or white cloth.

Catacombs Underground rooms and tunnels constructed by Roman Christians for the burial of their dead. The catacombs, which contain the remains of the early Roman martyrs' were used up to the period around 450 CE. Christians used to meet there to pray for their dead.

Catechesis (Greek *catechizein*, teach orally.) A journey of discovery made by teachers and students who share a common faith. Through catechesis young people or adult converts are introduced to the Christian faith.

Catechism A popular book containing the basic truths of Christianity in question-and-answer form.

Catechist A person who leads others to faith by reflection and example as well as instruction in the truths of the faith.

Catechumen A person who is learning about the faith before being baptised.

Catechumenate In the early days of the Church the catechumenate was the period when a person, who was going to be received into the Christian community, underwent suitable instruction before being baptised. The Second Vatican Council restored the catechumenate for adults as a time of preparation for the sacrament of Baptism.

Cathedral (Latin *cathedra*, chair.) The official church of a diocese where the bishop is the pastor. The cathedral church is where the bishop has his chair or throne. Cathedrals are usually large churches.

Cathedral

Catholic (Greek *catholikos*, universal, involving everybody.) A term used to describe the Roman Church. Members of the Roman Catholic Church are called Catholics. Members of other rites of the Catholic Church are also called Catholics, e.g. Maronite Catholics.

CE In the Common Era. This abbreviation is often used instead of AD. *See also* Anno Domini.

Celebrant Bishops, priests and deacons who preside at the Eucharist and other sacraments. In a real sense, all the people present are celebrants, because they all take part in the celebration.

Celibacy (Latin *caelebs*, unmarried.) The state of being unmarried. Priests belonging to the Roman rite, and members of religious orders, remain unmarried by taking a vow of celibacy as a sign of a special kind of dedication to service and the Kingdom of God.

Cenacle (Latin *cenaculum*, dining-room.) The upper room in Jerusalem where Jesus ate his last supper with his followers. He also appeared to the disciples after his resurrection in this room, and it was in the cenacle that the Holy Spirit came to the disciples at Pentecost.

Censer The metal cup or bowl in which lighted charcoal is placed. Onto this is sprinkled incense, which burns and gives off a scented smoke. It is used in liturgical ceremonies. The censer is hung from metal chains and is also called a thurible.

Centurion (Latin *centuria*, a division of 100.) An officer in the Roman Army who commanded 100 soldiers. Read about the centurion who had faith in Jesus (Matthew 8:5ff.).

Chalcedon A town near Istanbul in Turkey. In 451 CE a Church council was held there and proclaimed that Jesus Christ was truly God and truly human.

Chaldean rite Also called Assyrian or Persian rite, this is a liturgy of the Uniate Assyrians, which is conducted in the old Syriac language.

Chalice (Latin *calix*, cup.) A cup usually supported on a stem and base, and holding the wine to be consecrated at Mass. The chalice is considered sacred and so is crafted, selected and handled accordingly.

Chapel A small church other than the parish church or a small area of a larger church set apart for special devotion. In the Catholic tradition it often refers to the small room in which the Blessed Sacrament is kept.

Chapel of ease A chapel or small church built in a parish for those who live a long way from the parish church.

Chaplain A person appointed to minister to a special group of people, e.g. a school, hospital.

Charism *See* Gift.

Charismatic renewal (Greek *charisma*, free gift.) A movement in the Church by which people publicly claim to be ready to receive gifts from the Holy Spirit.

Chasuble A vestment or garment worn by priests and bishops over all other garments when they celebrate Mass. The colour of the chasuble changes to suit the liturgical season.

Chasuble

Choir (Greek *choros*, a band of singers and dancers.) (1) Part of a cathedral or church set aside for the recitation of the Divine Office by canons, monks, priests or members of religious orders. (2) A group of singers who sing sacred music at liturgical ceremonies and also lead the people in singing hymns, responses and parts of the Mass.

Chrism (Greek *chrisma*, anointing.) A mixture of olive oil and balm (or balsam) which is blessed by the bishop on Holy Thursday, and is used in conferring sacraments of baptism, Confirmation and Orders.

Chrismation Name of the sacrament of Confirmation in Eastern Catholic rites.

Christ (Greek *christos*, anointed one.) This word translates the Hebrew *messiah*. The title 'messiah' was given to all kings of Israel, because at their coronation they were anointed on the forehead with olive oil. This was a sign they had been specially chosen by God. Jesus is called Christ or Messiah because he is THE specially chosen king and Son of God who came to give life to his people.

Christening *See* Baptism.

Christian One who believes in Christ and follows his teaching.

Christian witness When Christians show, by the way they live, how much they love God and their fellow human beings, they give Christian witness. Jesus encouraged his followers to let their light shine before the world. This meant that they should lead good Christian lives and not be afraid to let others see their goodness and then give credit and praise to God.

Christmas (Old English *Cristes maesse*, the mass of Christ.) The feast that celebrates the birth of Jesus. The Christian Church placed the feast on 25 December, a date probably chosen to replace the pagan feast of the Roman sun god Sol Invictus.

Christology A branch of theology dealing with the person and life of Jesus Christ.

Church The first Christian communities

Church

were called gatherings or assemblies (in Greek, *ekklesia*). So a church was a gathering of those who were baptised. The Church is the whole body of Christians who follow Jesus in the way they live, worship and express their faith. The building where Christians gather to worship is also called a church.

Ciborium (Greek *kiborion*, cup.) In the liturgy it is the vessel in which the spiritual food of the Eucharist (i.e. the small host or particles of Blessed Sacrament) are kept for Holy Communion.

Circumcision (Latin *circumcisio*, a cutting around.) The removal of the male foreskin, i.e. the skin at the tip of the penis. Jewish boys were, and still are, circumcised eight days after birth. It is an outward sign of the special bond between them and God as members of the Jewish people.

Clergy (Latin *clericus*, priest.) The ordained ministers of the Church who are responsible for preaching, presiding at worship and liturgy, and the celebration of the sacraments, and serving the community in different kinds of ministry.

Collegiality The way in which the Pope and bishops form a body of ministers to make decisions and work together to lead and guide the Catholics of the world.

Colosseum A large circular entertainment arena in Rome where gladiator fights and other spectacles were held. It was opened in 80 CE and seated more that 80,000 people. According to tradition, many Christians died there as martyrs.

Colours, liturgical *See* Liturgical colours.

Commandments Laws which say how people should behave in their dealings with God and other human beings. The Ten Commandments are laws that Moses gave to the people of Israel (Exodus 20). They form the basis of the relationship or covenant between God and the people of Israel.

Communion (Latin *communio*, fellowship, a common sharing.) The eating and drinking of the body and blood of Christ. This action not only unites us with Jesus Christ, but also unites us with each other in the body of Christ. *See also* Eucharist and Fellowship.

Communion of saints The spiritual union between all Christians living and dead. 'Saints' in this expression means all Christians.

Communion service A ceremony in which communion is distributed without Mass being celebrated. An appointed person, not necessarily a priest, may distribute the body of Christ.

Communion under both species Reception of the body and blood of Christ under the forms of both bread and wine.

Community (1) A group of people who share the common idea of living, worshipping and working together in the way they follow Jesus Christ. (2) A religious community is a group of people who live the Christian life together under a special rule.

Compassion (Latin *compassio*, suffering with.) A feeling of sorrow or pity for the sufferings or misfortunes of others.

Compline The last prayer of the day in the Divine Office following Vespers. It is also called Night Prayer.

Concelebrant A priest who celebrates the Eucharist with one or more other priests. This used to be done frequently in the early days of the Church and is now returning as a common practice.

Conclave (Latin *con* with; *clavis* key.) The assembly of cardinals who gather to elect a Pope. The room in which they meet is also called the conclave.

Concluding rite The short rite at the end of Mass consisting of a greeting, the blessing and the dismissal.

Concordance A book containing an alphabetical list of all the principal words of the Bible together with the name of the book and the chapter and verse where each word occurs.

Concordat (Latin *concordare*, agree.) An official agreement between the government of a country and the Holy See that deals with matters concerning both group, e.g. the appointment of bishops, payment of priests.

Confession (Latin *confessio*, acknowledgment, confession.) Term for that part of the sacrament of Penance or Reconciliation where penitents tell the priest their sins and failings.

Confessional The name that was more commonly used in the past to describe the enclosed space where the priest and penitent celebrated the sacrament of Reconciliation. The confessional, or reconciliation room, is where the confession part of the first and second rites of Reconciliation is usually celebrated. Some confessionals have a screen that separates the priest and penitent. Others simply consist of a room where the two people sit face to face and celebrate the sacrament of Reconciliation together.

Confessor (1) A male saint who is not a martyr. (2) A priest who celebrates the sacrament of Reconciliation with the people, and who counsels those who take part in the sacrament.

Confirmation (Latin *confirmare*, make firm.) One of the sacraments of initiation by which baptised Christians receive the gifts of the Holy Spirit which strengthen them in their faith. During the ceremony of Confirmation the bishop or his representative anoints the foreheads of those being confirmed and calls on the Holy Spirit to come upon them.

Congregation (1) The people in a Christian community who are grouped together for worship. (2) A community of men or women who take simple vows of poverty, chastity and obedience, e.g. Sisters of Mercy, Christian Brothers.

Conscience That part of our mind and heart that tells us when a thing is right or wrong. I have a good conscience when I know that I am always trying to do the right thing and am sorry for the wrong things I have done. The Second Vatican Council declared that Christians are bound to follow their conscience faithfully.

Consecration (Latin *consecrare*, make something holy.) (1) A ceremony where any object or a building (e.g. a church) is specially blessed or set apart for a sacred use. (2) The solemn part of the Mass where the bread and wine become the body and blood of Christ.

Constantinople Former name for the city of Istanbul, the capital of Turkey. The city was first called Byzantium, but was renamed after the Emperor Constantine, who made it the capital city of the Roman Empire in the fourth century. It once rivalled Rome as the centre of Christianity. The Eastern Orthodox churches have their spiritual beginnings in Constantinople.

Contrition (Latin *contritus*, worn down, upset.) The sorrow that a person feels over past sins, together with the intention of not sinning again.

Conversion (Latin *convertere*, turn towards.) (1) A turning towards God by a sinner. (2) A turning towards the Church by a person who accepts its teachings and discipline.

Convert A person who changes his/her beliefs or religion.

Copt (Greek *aigyptos*, an Egyptian.) An Egyptian Christian who belongs to either the Catholic or Orthodox Coptic Church. The Copts are descendants of the native people of ancient Egypt.

Coptic rite The liturgy of the Coptic Church, which is the original Greek liturgy of Alexandria. It is celebrated in a form of the ancient Egyptian language with some elements of Arabic. The liturgy is long and slow, and contains a lot of solemn chanting.

Cornerstone When people built houses in ancient times, they started with four very large stones and put them at the four corners of the house. They then built the walls up around these very important stones. If the cornerstone was not strong the house would not be strong. Jesus is called the cornerstone of the Christian community because he is the foundation and the most important figure of the Church (Ephesians 2:20).

Corporal (Latin *corpus*, body.) A small white linen cloth (about 15 cm square) on which are placed the chalice and the sacred host during the celebration of the Eucharist.

Corpus Christi Latin for 'the body of Christ'. The feast day in honour of the presence of Christ in the Blessed Sacrament is celebrated each year on the Sunday after Trinity Sunday.

Cosmos (Greek *kosmos*, world, universe.) People in ancient times often believed that the universe was ruled by cosmic powers, i.e. good spirits and bad spirits.

Counter-Reformation The reformation or renewal of the Catholic Church in the sixteenth century. It was partly a reaction to the founding of the Protestant churches.

Covenant (Latin *convenire*, agree.) A binding agreement between two people or groups. Covenants in ancient times were generally not made in writing, as they are today, but when people gave their word, that was serious and binding. Covenants were made and sealed with a special ceremony, which bound the people to keep their promises. God made a covenant with the people of Israel, which meant that they would be God's special people and would remain faithful to God. In return, God promised to protect this chosen people. Christians bind themselves to Jesus in the new covenant through Baptism.

Creation God, the creator, made the world out of nothing. People in ancient times told stories to try to explain that the universe was made by their god(s). The Hebrew people also had stories of creation, which contain details that they borrowed from the people of Mesopotamia. A Hebrew creation story is found in the Bible (Genesis 1). This story does not try to say HOW God created the world, but sets out to show that there is only one God who is the creator of everything.

Credence table A small table in the sanctuary of a church that holds whatever is needed for liturgical functions.

Creed (Latin *credere*, trust, believe.) A statement of belief in the church's main teachings. Creeds were generally used in the liturgy because Christians felt the need to express their belief in ceremonial form. *See also* Apostles' Creed and Nicene Creed.

Crosier An ornamental staff carried by the bishop as a sign of his responsibility to look after the faithful of his diocese.

Cross (Latin *crux*, cross.) Because Jesus was executed on a cross, it has become the chief symbol of the Christian faith throughout the ages. We make the sign of the cross as a reminder that Jesus died for us on a cross. *See* Crucifixion.

Crucifix A cross with an image of Christ attached or painted on it.

Crucifixion A form of punishment invented by the Persians and used by the Romans to execute people guilty of serious crimes, such as murder, robbery, treason, rebellion. The criminal was stripped, then roped or nailed to a T-shaped cross and left to die of exposure, hunger, thirst and suffocating cramps.

Cruet

Cruet A small vessel or jug used at Mass to hold the water or wine.

Crusade An expedition undertaken by armies of Christians from Europe in the eleventh, twelfth and thirteenth centuries, in order to win back the Holy Land from the Arab Muslims. These military campaigns were fought under the banner of the cross.

Crypt (Greek *kryptos*, hidden.) The room or vault beneath the main floor of a church used as a burial place.

Curate (Latin *curator*, one who cares.) The priest who is assistant to the parish priest.

Curia (Latin *curia*, senate-house.) The groups (congregations) and people who form the centre of government for the Catholic Church and assist the Pope and bishops. Every diocese has its own curia.

Crucifix

Dark Ages Period in Europe from the fifth century to the eleventh century. It is called the Dark Ages because it followed the destruction of the Roman Empire.

Deacon (Greek *diakonos*, servant, minister.) (1) A minister of the early Christian Church who looked after the daily business of the community. (2) A minister ordained to assist the bishop (permanent deacon) or as a step leading towards priesthood. *See also* Permanent deacon.

Deaconess Title of women in the early Church who assisted the minister and performed special works and duties in the Christian community, e.g. anointing of women at Baptism, visiting the sick and needy. The order of deaconess had dropped out of the church's ministry by the eleventh century. There are modern orders of deaconesses in some Protestant churches.

Dead Sea A salty lake formed by the inflow of the Jordan River into a very deep valley, which is 20 km east of Jerusalem. The Dead Sea is too salty to support marine life. It is 80 km long, 18 km at its widest point, and is about 400 m below the level of the Mediterranean. Its deepest part is also about 400 m.

Dead Sea Scrolls A scroll is a document written on parchment or paper and rolled onto one or two rods or spindles. The Dead Sea Scrolls, which date back to the first and second centuries BCE, consist of some books of scripture and other documents that had been copied by a religious community who lived together at Qumran on the shores of the Dead Sea. When the Romans attacked Qumran in 68 CE, the members of the community put their precious scrolls in earthenware jars and hid them in caves in the cliffs nearby. This was to prevent the Romans from destroying the sacred writings. Some of these scrolls were accidentally discovered by local Arab shepherds in 1947. The scrolls tell us a lot about the way of life of the Qumran community, and also tell us that all the books of the Hebrew scriptures had been composed before the first century BCE.

Dean Priest appointed by the bishop to have special responsibility for a group of parishes called a deanery.

Death The end of life. Jewish belief about death and afterlife evolved slowly over centuries with the unfolding of divine revelation. In many sections of the Hebrew scriptures (Old Testament) we find the belief expressed that the 'spirit' departed when a person died. The dead person continued to exist as an individual in Sheol, but was incapable of any activity. Later, people began to believe in a personal resurrection as life with God when they thought about God's way of rewarding good people and punishing bad people. In the New Testament turning away from God is seen as a type of death. Through baptism, Christians die with Christ to all evil, and so have the promise of rising with him to new life.

Decalogue (Greek *deka*, ten; *logos*, word, rule, law.) The Ten Commandments given to the people of Israel by Moses (Exodus 20). *See also* Commandments.

Denarius A Roman silver coin. In Jesus' time it was worth a day's pay for a labourer.

Desecration Seriously disrespectful treatment of something that is sacred.

Devil *See* Satan.

Devotion A particular attraction towards some Christian mystery or person, e.g. people who are attracted to the Mother of God may pray to Mary every day as a sign of their devotion to her.

Diaspora A Greek word meaning 'a scattering'. It refers to the Jewish people who live in Gentile lands outside of

Palestine. It was the existence of Jewish communities in diaspora that prompted the Septuagint and the development of the synagogue.

Didache A Greek word meaning 'teaching'. A short Christian book from the first or second century made up of two parts: (1) moral teachings that describe how Christians ought to behave; and (2) a set of directions concerning the work and responsibilities of Church ministers.

Diocese (Greek *dioikesis*, housekeeping, district.) The people and district under the authority of a bishop.

Disciple (Latin *discipulus*, learner, pupil.) A person who follows a teacher. Most philosophers and religious teachers had disciples in ancient times. Those who followed Jesus were called the disciples. All believers in Jesus may be called disciples.

Dispensation (Latin *dispensare*, weigh, hand out.) A special permission excusing someone from having to obey a law.

Divine (Latin *divinus*, godlike.) Connected with God; characteristic of God.

Divine Liturgy Name for the prayers, hymns and ceremonies that make up the service of the Eucharist in the Eastern Catholic rites and Orthodox churches.

Divine Office The official public and common prayer of the church. It consists of psalms, readings, hymns and prayers that are recited or sung, as an act of praise to God, at certain hours of every day of the year. The Divine Office consists of Morning Prayer (Lauds), Evening Prayer (Vespers), Night Prayer (Compline), the Office of Readings (Matins) and several shorter hours called Prayer during the Day. Members of religious communities usually sing or recite the Divine Office together, while most priests recite it privately. Lay people are also encouraged to take part in the Divine Office by reciting it from a breviary. *See* Breviary.

Divorce (Latin *divortium*, separation.) A formal separation of a husband and wife. Jesus discouraged divorce because it was against God's original plan and broke up a sacred agreement between two people (Matthew 19:3–9).

Docetism (Greek *dokein*, seem, appear.) A false teaching in the early Church which said that Jesus was not really a man, but only appeared to be one.

Doctors of the church A title given to teachers and writers in the Church who are noted for their learning and holiness of life, e.g. St Thomas Aquinas, St Teresa of Avila.

Doctrine (Latin *doctrina*, teaching) Something that is taught. An individual teaching or a collection of teachings. The doctrine of the Church includes the beliefs and teachings that are based on the person and work of Jesus.

Dogma (Greek *dogma*, a fixed opinion.) An article of faith that is part of the solemn teaching of the Popes and Ecumenical Councils. For example, the teaching that Jesus Christ is both God and man is a dogma of the church.

Doxology (Greek *doxa*, glory.) A prayer giving glory to God, e.g. 'Glory be to the Father and to the Son and to the Holy Spirit'.

Drachma A Greek silver coin equal to one Roman denarius.

Easter The greatest feast of the Church year, which celebrates the rising of Jesus Christ from the dead. In Europe, Easter replaced an ancient spring festival during which people honoured Eostre, the goddess of dawn or spring, and exchanged gifts of eggs, which symbolised life. The people also lit fires, which were symbols of new life.

Easter Triduum The three days that celebrate the passion, death and resurrection of Jesus Christ. It begins with the Mass of the Lord's Supper on Holy Thursday evening and closes on Easter Sunday evening.

Easter vigil The liturgical ceremonies held on Holy Saturday evening in which Christ is remembered as the Son of God who died and rose from the dead. The ceremonies and readings remind us that God intended all along to send Jesus to show us the way to salvation. The Easter readings focus on Christ's sacrifice and God's loving nature, and the Eucharist celebrates Christ's presence among us. The Easter fire and the paschal candle represent Christ who brings new life to the world. The baptismal water, which is blessed during the vigil ceremony, is a symbol of Baptism, through which Christians die with Christ to sin and rise with him to a new, grace-filled life.

Eastern churches Groups of Christian churches whose laws, customs and rites are based on the practices of Christianity in the Middle East and Eastern Europe. Some of these churches are united to the Roman Catholic Church and some are not. They have their own distinctive canon law, ceremonies and sacraments. Those united to Rome are called Uniate churches. Those not united to Rome belong to two groups: (1) the Orthodox Eastern churches, and (2) the Nestorian, Armenian, Coptic, Ethiopic and Syrian Jacobite churches. *See also* Rite.

Ecclesia (Greek *ekklesia*, assembly gathering.) Early Christian groups called themselves 'assemblies', e.g. the assembly at Rome, the assembly at Corinth. Later the word 'church' came to be used in place of assembly. The Christian assembly is a sign by which people show to the world that they have faith in Jesus Christ and recognise the presence of God among them. *See also* Church.

Ecclesiology A branch of theology dealing with the study of the history, structure and mission of the Church.

Ecology (Greek *oikos*, house, place where a family lives.) A branch of biology that deals with the balance of relationships between all creatures and their environment. Responsible human beings have a respect for all things in creation realising that it goes against God's wishes when we pollute or destroy our environment.

Ecumenical Movement (ecumenism) (Greek *oikoumenikos*, universal.) A series of activities that are aimed at promoting the unity of Christian churches.

Egypt (Ancient Egyptian *hi-ku-Ptah*, house of [the god] Ptah.) A land in north-west Africa that contained one of the most powerful civilisations of ancient times. Some of the tribes of Israel moved to Egypt around the seventeenth century BCE, and after some time were made slaves by the Egyptians. The book of Exodus tells how the people of Israel, with Moses as their leader, escaped from Egypt under the protection of God.

Elder Senior men of a tribe or town. In ancient times, older people were greatly respected for their experience and wisdom. In the Hebrew scriptures the elders: (1) represented the people in political and religious activities; (2) advised the ruler of the tribe or town; (3) acted as judges in court. In the New Testament the elders were the senior men in each assembly who made important decisions, and made sure there was order all the time. Later, the bishops were chosen from among the elders. *See also* Bishop.

Elect Chosen. St Paul calls his fellow Christians 'the chosen ones'. The Christian community are the elect because they have been called by God to follow Jesus Christ and to spread the good news of salvation to the world.

Election, Papal The process by which a Pope is elected. A majority of two-thirds plus one of the cardinals of the conclave is needed.

Emmanuel or Immanuel (Hebrew *immanu*, with us; *el*, God.) This word describes the Messiah, who is God with us. The prophet Isaiah originally called King Hezekiah 'Emmanuel' (Isaiah 7:14), and Christians talk of Jesus when they use the word, because he, more than anyone else, is God with us.

Encyclical (Greek *enkyklios*, circular.) A general letter addressed by the Pope to all the bishops and people of the Church.

Entrance rite *See* Introductory rites.

Entrance song The song or psalm that is sung as the priest and ministers enter the church. If there is no singing, the special verse in the missal is recited by the people or by a reader.

Ephesus A town in south-eastern Turkey which was a major Christian centre in the first five centuries. The Church council which declared Mary to be the Mother of God, was held there in 431 CE.

Epiphany (Greek *epiphaneia*, appearance.) The feast celebrated on 6 January, which commemorates the visit of the Magi to Jesus. In Australia, Epiphany is celebrated on the Sunday nearest 6 January. It is sometimes called Twelfth Night, since it is twelve days after Christmas. The feast celebrates the appearance of God on earth. In the Eastern churches Epiphany commemorates the baptism of Jesus.

Episcopal conference A gathering of the bishops of a country, or several countries, for the purpose of discussing and sharing ideas on how they can best look after the educational, devotional and pastoral needs of the people in their dioceses.

Episcopalian Church The Anglican Church in the United States, which is governed by bishops who are elected by the priests and lay representatives.

Epistle (Greek *epistole*, written communication.) A letter intended to be read aloud to a whole group of people. The letters in the New Testament were written to encourage groups of Christians to keep their faith and lead good lives. The writers of the epistles deal with the various questions and problems that the first Christian communities had to cope with.

Eschatology (Greek *eschatos*, final, end.) That part of theology dealing with final things or the end-time: death, the second coming of Jesus Christ (the *parousia*), judgement, purgatory, heaven, hell.

Essenes A community of Jewish people who lived a strict life of work, prayer and study. They date from the second century before Jesus Christ. Some of them married, but most of them remained celibate. It is generally believed that their headquarters were at Qumran, on the western shore of the Dead Sea, but many of them lived in groups scattered in towns and villages. Their leader was called 'the Teacher of Righteousness'. They believed that they were the truly faithful ones and that the rest of the Jews were not keeping the law properly. They were waiting for the coming of the Messiah and the kingdom of God. Their community buildings were destroyed by the Romans in 70 CE. *See also* Dead Sea Scrolls.

Ethics (Greek *ethikos*, good, moral.) A set of standards for judging whether an action is right or wrong. For instance, in businesses and professions there are standards and values that people can use to decide on the proper way of acting towards the clients they deal with.

Ethiopian Church The Church founded by a small group of Christian Ethiopians, descendants of those who migrated from southern Arabia to Africa. The Church was founded from Alexandria in northern Egypt, probably around the middle of the fourth century. The Ethiopic rite is a form of the Coptic liturgy in the Ge'ez language, a long-dead Semitic tongue.

Eucharist (Greek *eucharistia*, thanksgiving.) This word first appears in Christian writing late in the first century. In the New Testament, the meeting at which the Christians gathered in order to remember Jesus' death and resurrection was called the Lord's Supper and later became known as the Eucharist. The sacrament of the Eucharist is the celebration of the death and resurrection of Christ in the Mass and is the central act of worship of the Catholic community. Eucharist also refers to the consecrated bread and wine. *See* Blessed Sacrament.

Eucharistic Prayer That part of the Mass that begins with the Preface, after the 'Holy, holy, holy', and ends with the Great Amen just before the Our Father. The Eucharistic Prayer contains prayers of praise, thanksgiving, acclamation, the words of consecration, prayers of remembrance for the living and the dead, and prayers of offering. *See* Preface.

Euthanasia (Greek *euthanasia*, a well-ordered or easy death.) The deliberate killing of a person who is suffering great pain or an incurable disease. The Catholic Church condemns euthanasia because it goes against the sacredness of all human life that comes from God.

Evangelical Evangelical means 'according to the Gospel' and is the name given to Protestant churches that believe in the doctrines contained in the Apostles' Creed, and place greater emphasis on the teaching and authority of the scriptures than on the traditions of the Church itself.

Evangelise To teach people about Jesus Christ as saviour, with a view to converting them to the Christian faith.

Evangelist (Greek *euangelion*, good news.) (1) One who preaches the good news that Jesus has saved us. (2) The writer of a gospel. Matthew, Mark, Luke and John are the four evangelists.

Examination of conscience The act of recalling the sins we have committed. It is usual to have an examination of conscience as part of the sacrament of Penance or Reconciliation.

Excommunicate (Latin *excommunicare*, put out of the community.) To cut someone off or to cut oneself off from being a member of the Church or receiving the sacraments. The excommunication of a member of the Church is an extremely rare occurrence.

Exile Being away from one's country or home for a long period. The Jewish people were twice conquered and taken into captivity: the northern kingdom (capital, Samaria) by the Assyrians in 721 BCE, and the southern kingdom (capital, Jerusalem) by the Babylonians in 587 BCE. The political purpose of the exile was to prevent an uprising in Jerusalem and to help the economy in Babylon. Many Jewish people at the time believed that this exile was a punishment by God for the wrongs they had committed.

Exodus (Greek *exodos*, departure, exit.) This refers to the departure of the Hebrew people from slavery in Egypt (probably in the thirteenth century BCE). Under the protection of God and the leadership of Moses, they left Egypt and travelled through the Sinai Desert to Canaan. The Book of Exodus tells this story. The exodus from slavery has become the most important event in the history of Israel, because it marked the beginning of the nation, and is the symbol for God's salvation of the people of Israel.

Exorcise (Greek *exorkizein*, put someone under oath.) To drive out an evil spirit with prayers and solemn ceremonies.

Exorcist A priest who exorcises.

Faith (Hebrew *aman*, be firm, true; Latin *fides*, trust, confidence.) (1) In the Hebrew scriptures, God was always true to the people of Israel and was called the Faithful One. In the Christian writings, faith was the way people let go of self-interest and believed in Jesus and his teachings, and then remained faithful to them. Faith is a gift from God that allows people to believe and trust in the love and protection of God. (2) A system of religious belief: the Jewish faith, the Christian faith.

Fast To go without eating or to eat little for a period of time. Among the people of Israel this was done as a mark of sorrow for sin as well as an act of devotion. For the early Christians, fasting usually accompanied prayer when a person wanted God's help for something important. Today, people sometimes fast (e.g. during the season of Lent) as a form of penance or self-discipline. In the Roman rite, Ash Wednesday and Good Friday are days of fasting for those between fifteen and sixty years of age.

Fathers of the church A name given to important teachers and bishops who defended the truths of the Church in early Christian times. Sometimes they are called Latin or Greek Fathers, depending on where they came from. For example, St Ambrose was a Latin Father and St John Chrysostom was a Greek Father.

Fatima A small town in Portugal where Mary is believed to have appeared to three children between 1915 and 1917. It is now a popular place of pilgrimage.

Feast day (Latin *festum*, holiday, festival.) A day of celebration commemorating a saint, a teaching or an event of religious importance.

Fellowship The quality of sharing and companionship in a community. Members of the Christian community share friendship, faith, their possessions and respect for each other. Christians share their happiness and sadness. They also share the life of Christ.

Feminist Theology The study of God and human relations with God that is based on the idea that women are equal to men. Feminist theologians understand that women have been disadvantaged and deprived of their full power and dignity by the domination of males in human society throughout the centuries. This male domination has been, and still is, a mark of the Christian churches. Feminist theologians try to bring the experience of women to the practical life of the Church and to the study of theology.

First Communion The reception of the body and blood of Jesus Christ for the first time.

Flesh In the scriptures, flesh refers to human beings and human nature. In the New Testament the 'flesh' is often used to describe sinful human nature that is opposed to the human nature redeemed by the grace of Christ. To walk in the flesh is the opposite of walking in the Spirit, and means to lead a life of sin.

Forgiveness Pardon given for an offence. A clue to what forgiveness means can be seen in the three beautiful Hebrew words which can be translated as 'forgiveness': *kipper*, cover; *nasa*, lift up and carry away; *salach*, let go. In forgiveness, the hurt or offence is let go and carried away, so that there is no longer a wall between people and God. The Hebrew people turned to God to pray for forgiveness, and God always forgave sinners who asked for pardon. For Christians, forgiveness is obtained through the death of Jesus Christ (Ephesians 1:7). Christians are also urged to forgive one another (Matthew 6:14).

Fraction rite (Latin *fractio*, breaking.) The breaking of the consecrated host at Mass by the celebrant. It is accompanied by the singing or reciting of the 'Lamb of God', and recalls the action of Jesus when he broke bread and gave it to his disciples at the Last Supper. It also symbolises that we, who are many, are made one when we receive Communion.

Free will The ability of human beings to make choices in life without being forced by anybody else or by anything in themselves.

Friar (Latin *frater*, brother.) A member of one of the male religious orders that used to rely on begging for their daily food, e.g. Franciscan friar.

Friends, Society of A Christian group called 'Quakers'. At their prayer meetings, anyone who feels inspired by the Spirit may speak out. Quakers are opposed to all forms of violence.

Fundamentalism In Christianity, fundamentalism is a religious movement which insists that the Bible must be understood and believed word for word without interpretation. The official Catholic teaching says that the Bible, as a whole, contains the truths that God wants us to know for our salvation. It also recognises that some sections of the Bible contain poetry and creative imagery that are meant to be interpreted symbolically. The name comes from a set of paperback volumes called *The Fundamentals: a Testimony of Truth*. These were written between 1910 and 1915 by a group of Bible teachers who believed that modern liberal culture was attacking the truths of the Christian faith. The fundamentalists insisted that the Bible contains no error, not only with regard to matters of faith and Christian teaching, but also to matters of science, history and geography.

Gehenna Hebrew name for the valley separating ancient Jerusalem from the hills to the south. The ancient Canaanites used to offer human sacrifice by fire there, so it became known as a place of punishment by fire for those who were wicked during their lives.

General intercessions *See* Prayer of the faithful.

Genesis A Greek word for 'beginning'. The Book of Genesis is the first book in the Bible and deals with the beginnings of the world and of the Hebrew people.

Gentile (Latin *gentilis*, foreigner, heathen.) Word used by Jews to describe anybody who is not a Jew.

Genuflection (Latin *genuflectere*, bend the knee.) A bending of the knee which is a mark of reverence for Jesus in the Blessed Sacrament.

Gethsemane (Aramaic *gat shemene*, oil press.) The olive grove just outside the walls of Jerusalem where Jesus went to pray after the Last Supper and where he was arrested.

Gift Christians used the Greek word *charisma* to refer to a gift from God that is freely given and does not depend on what people deserve. This kind of gift-giving does not depend on anything in return. All Christians have gifts from the Spirit, and these enable them to live their lives for others. *See also* Grace.

Gifts of the Holy Spirit Special gifts which enable us to be guided by the Holy Spirit, who unites all Christians in love. These gifts are wisdom, understanding, knowledge, counsel, fortitude, piety and fear of the Lord.

Glory The splendour or magnificence of God. For the Israelites the glory of God was seen in the way God looked after Israel. In the New Testament people give glory to God by acknowledging the wonderful nature of God.

Gnostic (Greek *gnosis*, knowledge.) A member of a religious group claiming to have superior knowledge of spiritual things. Gnostics were heretics who believed that this knowledge would bring about their salvation. They did not believe that Jesus was a real human being because his body was not real. They believed that the physical world was evil.

Gnostic Gospels Sayings and stories of Jesus contained in documents that belonged to groups of early Christians called Gnostics. Because they contain ideas which do not agree with all the teachings in the gospels of Matthew, Mark, Luke and John, these gospels (e.g. the Gospel of Thomas) were never accepted as part of scripture by the majority of Christians.

Godparent The prefix 'god' comes from Old English. It is a sign that there is a spiritual relationship between the godparent and the person being baptised. The godparent is one who speaks for a person who is being baptised. The godparent must be at least fourteen years of age, and already baptised. The godparent may not be father or mother, or wife or husband of the person being baptised. Godparents accept some responsibility for the religious education of a person who is baptised.

Golgotha Aramaic word meaning 'the place of the skull'. The place where criminals were executed outside the city of Jerusalem in the time of Jesus. Jesus himself was crucified there. *See also* Calvary.

Good (Greek *agathos*, good in a moral sense; *kalos*, morally good, beautiful and precious.) Genuine Christian goodness is lovely to experience (unlike some forms of goodness that can be unattractive).

Good Friday The Friday of Holy Week when Christians remember the suffering and death of Jesus Christ on the cross. Mass cannot be celebrated on this day, but Holy Communion is distributed to the people. There are special readings and prayers, including the Passion story in St John's Gospel. The cross is also venerated by the people.

Gospel (Old English *godspell*, good news.) (1) Used by early Christians to describe the good news that Jesus saved us from the power of evil. (2) In the New Testament there are four versions of the good news called gospels.

Grace (Latin *gratia,* favour, pleasantness, thanks.) (1) The gift that God freely gives people to enable them to lead good lives. Human beings have been saved by the kindness or grace of God (Ephesians 2:5). Actual grace is given by God as a help for particular human actions. Sanctifying grace is the presence of God within a person. (2) Christians should treat other people with grace or loving-kindness (Colossians 4:6); God has shown great favour or grace to Mary (Luke 1:30). *See also* Gift.

Grace at meals A prayer thanking God for the food that has been prepared and asking a blessing on the food and those who are gathered to eat it.

Great Amen At the end of the Eucharistic Prayer at Mass the celebrant chants or recites a prayer giving glory to God, which begins: 'Through him, with him and in him ...' The people respond to this prayer by saying or singing 'Amen'. This is the Great Amen and through it the people express their agreement with all the prayers and actions that have gone before it.

Great Schism (Greek *schisma*, split.) A term used for two separate events: (1) the break between the Western Church (Rome) and the Eastern Church (Constantinople) in 1054; (2) the period in Europe between 1378 and 1417 when there were two, and even three, rival Popes at the one time. There was a Pope in Rome and a rival in the French city of Avignon, each claiming to be the rightful Pope. This schism arose out of political differences among five European countries.

Greek Orthodox Church The national Greek Church, which uses the Byzantine rite. *See also* Byzantine rite.

Gregorian Chant Also called Plainchant or Plainsong. It is vocal music with a single melody used in sung prayer and worship. This form of singing comes from the chants of the ancient Mediterranean world and has been named after Pope Gregory I (ca. 540–604), who put together and arranged a collection of these chants.

Guardian Angel An angel who protects each one of us from spiritual and bodily harm. Belief in the Guardian Angel is a Christian devotion and not a defined dogma of the church.

Hades   Greek name for the abode of the dead. In ancient Greek literature Hades was the underworld where people went after death.

Hail Mary   A prayer in honour of the Blessed Virgin Mary. The first half of the Hail Mary quotes the greetings given to Mary by the angel Gabriel and St Elizabeth (Luke 1:28, 42).

Halleluia   *see* Alleluia

Hallowed   (Old English *hallow*, make holy.) By holy, the ancient Hebrews meant great, wonderful, majestic, mysterious. The expression 'hallowed be thy name' in the Our Father means 'may your name be made holy'.

Hasidim   (Hebrew *hesed*, loyalty.) The Hasidim were the holy ones who were loyal to their responsibilities to God. They stood out as a distinct group in Judaism because they were strict about keeping the law. Today, such strict or orthodox Jews (the men usually wear black hats and long black coats) are still called Hasidim.

Heart   Among the Hebrew people the heart was the centre of all feelings and inspiration. Humans were in touch with God with the heart. All plans, thoughts, attitudes, fears and hopes came from the heart. People who love God with all their heart are able to be generous and unselfish towards God and other people.

Heaven   A state of complete and unlimited happiness that has no end. This happiness comes from being with God and seeing God face to face. The fullness of heavenly happiness is the reward given to those who lead good lives here on earth.

Hebrew   There is no certain knowledge about the origin of the word, but there is the suggestion that it comes from *habiru*, which means 'from across the water'. Hebrews are the Jewish people descended from Eber, son of Shem. Abraham is revered as the father of the Hebrew people. The Hebrew language belongs to the Semitic group, which includes Arabic, and is closely related to the Canaanite language. Modern Hebrew is the official language of the modern state of Israel.

Hebrew scriptures   The sacred writings of the Hebrew people. The authors of these writings were inspired by God to write about the truths that God wanted to reveal to the people of Israel. Christians often refer to the Hebrew scriptures as the Old Testament. *See* Old Testament.

Hell   (German *hel*, hole, place of the dead.) A state of painful separation from God. When Jesus spoke about hell he used the ideas that were common in Jewish religion of his time. For example, he said that hell was like being in dark place, or being thrown into a fire (Matthew 8:12; 18:9), where sinful people would be cut off from the happiness and goodness of God. Jesus said that it was possible for people to turn away from God by rejecting goodness and by not caring for others (Matthew 25:41–46). Such people cut themselves off from God and choose punishment. *See also* Gehenna.

Help of Christians   Mary is called the Help of Christians because of the assistance she gives to those who pray for her help. Our Lady Help of Christians is the chief patron of Australia. The feast day of Our Lady Help of Christians is 24 May.

Heresy/Heretics   (Greek *haeresis*, a party, sect.) The teachings of a group that are different from the teachings of a religion or church. The earliest Christians were called 'heretics', a sect of Judaism. In later Christianity any false teaching was called heresy. The followers of a heresy are called heretics.

Hermeneutics   (Greek *hermeneuo*, to interpret.) The science of understanding or interpreting the meaning of the scriptures.

Herodians Those people in the time of Christ who supported the rule of King Herod in Judea, and the Roman rule on which it depended. They were opposed by the Zealots. *See* Zealots.

Hierarchy (Greek *hiera* sacred; *arche* rule.) A body of officials organised in ranks and orders. In the Catholic Church the hierarchy is made up of the Pope and the bishops under his authority.

High Priest Israelite priests served at shrines and the Temple in Jerusalem. They offered sacrifices and organised sacred ceremonies. The High Priest was the chief priest, who usually inherited the office from his father. He was the most important person in the Jewish community, and was president of the committee of religious rulers called the Sanhedrin.

Hinduism (Persian *hind*, belonging to India.) The dominant religion of India that came out of the teachings of the sacred writings called the Vedas. Hinduism evolved in about the fifth century BCE, but there are many groups within the religion and there is no common set of dogmas. The many gods of Hinduism are expressions and manifestations of the supreme god Brahman.

Holocaust (Greek *holokauston*, whole burnt offering.) (1) A sacrifice offered to God in which the victim is completely burned by fire. (2) The name given to the planned destruction of the Jewish people in Europe by the Nazis between 1933 and 1945, when six million Jews were murdered.

Holy In the Hebrew scriptures God is holy because God is wonderful, magnificent and far better than any human being. The Israelites called themselves a 'holy people' because they were associated with Yahweh. Jesus is not often called holy (Mark 1:24). People are considered to be holy when they turn away from evil and their lives are filled with love for God and other people. All Christians are called by God to lives of love and holiness (Colossians 3:12). *See also* Saint.

Holy Communion *See* Communion.

Holy Cross (1) The cross on which Jesus was crucified. It is venerated by Christians because of the key part it played in Jesus' work in salvation. In the Roman rite the cross is venerated by the people during the Good Friday liturgy. (2) A season of the Armenian, Maronite and Syrian rites when people celebrate the victory of Jesus over death and evil through his suffering and death on the cross.

Holy days Days that are set aside so that people may celebrate a feast day in a special way, e.g. attendance at Mass. They are called days of obligation because Catholics are obliged to take part in the celebration of the Eucharist on these days. The holy days of obligation in Australia are: all Sundays, Christmas Day, Ascension Thursday (celebrated on Sunday in Australia), Assumption (15 August), All Saints (1 November).

Holy Family The family of Nazareth consisting of Joseph, Mary and Jesus. The Holy Family is seen by Christians as the model of good and happy family life.

Holy Father The title of respect given to the Pope, who is the spiritual father of the Roman Catholic Church.

Holy, holy, holy The acclamation that follows the Preface at Mass. It is a prayer of praise, based on the praises offered to God by the angels that are quoted in Isaiah 6, and marks the beginning of the Eucharistic Prayer. It recalls the praise offered to Jesus by the crowd when he entered Jerusalem (Mark 11:1–10).

Holy hour An hour of prayer and devotions generally before the Blessed Sacrament.

Holy Land Palestine or the modern state of Israel. It is called holy because it is the land in which Jesus lived and moved during his life.

Holy of Holies The holiest place; the innermost sanctuary of the Temple in Jerusalem. It was a dark, empty room which represented the presence of God among the people. The High Priest entered this room once a year on the Day of Atonement to pray for the forgiveness of all the sins of the people.

Holy Orders Properly called the Sacrament of Orders which is conferred on those members of the Catholic community who are called by God to serve the whole community as deacons, priests and bishops. All members of the Christian community are called to minister to each other, but Orders sets certain people apart for specialised ministries, such as proclaiming the word of God, presiding at the Eucharist and the forgiveness of sins, and working for the unity and spiritual growth of the community.

Holy Saturday The day before Easter Sunday and part of the Easter Triduum.

Holy See (Latin *sedes*, seat, centre.) A see is the area, or diocese, ruled by the bishop. The Holy See is the diocese of the Pope as Bishop of Rome.

Holy Sepulchre The tomb in which Jesus was buried. At present there is a church built over the site traditionally regarded as the place where Jesus was buried. This Church of the Holy Sepulchre is shared by the Franciscans and the Eastern churches of the Greeks, Copts, Syrians and Armenians.

Holy Spirit (Latin *spiritus*, breath, breeze.) The Hebrews used the word *ruah*, meaning breath or wind, to describe the Spirit of God as a force that gives life and help to creatures. It creates, saves and gives inspiration to human beings. In the New Testament the Holy Spirit is the power of God that inspires or gives good ideas to Jesus and his followers. The Spirit sanctifies Christians and helps them to live according to the teachings of Jesus, to pray, and to be united to God. The Holy Spirit inspires and guides the Church community in all its activities. In Christian theology, the Holy Spirit is the third person of the Trinity. *See also* Paraclete.

Holy Thursday Thursday in Holy Week. The liturgy of Holy Thursday evening commemorates the Last Supper of Jesus and his disciples, when he washed their feet and celebrated the first Eucharist. *See also* Maundy Thursday.

Holy Water Water that becomes a sacred sign after it has been blessed by a priest. It is used for blessings and sprinkling at Mass. It is used by Christians, when they enter and leave a church, to sign the cross on themselves, as a reminder of their baptism. The use of holy water is also a sign of washing and cleanliness.

Holy Week The week before Easter Sunday. It is the last week of Lent, and recalls the suffering of Jesus Christ. It begins on Passion or Palm Sunday and ends with the beginning of the Easter Triduum.

Holy year A year in which the Pope grants special spiritual favours. It is usually celebrated every twenty-five years.

Homily (Greek *homilia*, lecture, instruction.) A short instruction or reflection which opens up the meaning of the scriptures and their application to the Christian life.

Holy Land

Hope   Through the virtue of hope, Christians are optimists who trust that they will take part in the final peace and happiness of God promised to those who are faithful to the teachings of Jesus Christ. To hope is to trust that in spite of all the hurt and brokenness that may happen, the love of God will win in the end.

Hosanna   (Hebrew *hoshiyah na*, save us, we ask.) A response said by the people of Israel, particularly at the Temple ceremony on the Feast of Booths. It later became a cry which was to accompany the arrival of the Messiah.

Host   (Latin *hostia*, animal used in sacrifice.) The word applied to the bread that is consecrated in the celebration of the Eucharist. It refers to the sacrifice of Jesus.

Humanism   A way of thinking that gives importance to human beings and human concerns. There are two kinds of humanism. One kind believes in God while the other does not. The kind of humanism that has no place for God believes that human beings are the most important consideration in the universe. Christian humanism believes that human beings reach their full dignity when they have a proper relationship with God.

Hymn   (Greek *hymnos*, a song in praise of gods or heroes.) A poem honouring God, which is set to music. The Psalms are Hebrew hymns, i.e. songs meant to be sung at festivals, in processions, during worship in the Temple, etc. They give praise and thanks to God. The Christians also sang Psalms and made up their own hymns about God and Jesus Christ (Acts 16:25; Ephesians 5:19). Christians have been composing and singing a great many hymns right up to the present time.

Hypocrite   (Greek *hypokrites*, actor.) Hypocrites are people who pretend to be what they are not. In the gospels, Jesus attacked some of the Scribes and Pharisees for being hypocrites, that is, 'pretending to be good'. Jesus was really attacking their malice and craftiness.

Icon (Greek *eikon*, picture.) A religious image painted on a flat surface. The icon reminds people of the person whose image is painted on it, and it is a help to their devotion and prayer. The Eastern churches do not have statues, and so icons are very important to them.

Iconoclasts People who want to destroy all images and statues in churches, because they are afraid that people will become superstitious and put their faith in pictures and statues.

Iconostasis The screen used in the Eastern churches to separate the sanctuary from the main part of the church. It is decorated with icons and is the distinguishing feature of Eastern Church buildings.

Idol (Greek *eidolon*, image, likeness.) An image of a god that is worshipped. The Israelites were strictly forbidden to make any images of humans or animals so that they would not be tempted to pray to idols instead of to the one true God.

Idolatry The worship of false gods generally represented by idols, such as statues or carvings. People can make idols out of money, power, personal reputation, etc.

IHS An abbreviation for the Greek name for Jesus, IHSOUS (pronounced Yesus).

Image of God Humans are made in the image of God (Genesis 1:26). The Greek word for image is *eikon* (from which comes the word 'echo'), which means 'of the very stuff'. Being in God's image, human beings can have a loving relationship with God and can grow in the likeness of God. For St Paul, it was Jesus who was most like God (2 Corinthians 4:4).

Imitation of Christ (1) Living the Christian life, with its joys and sufferings, after the example given by Jesus. (2) A popular devotional book written by a monk, Thomas à Kempis, in about 1400. It has been used by millions of people as an inspiration and help in following Christ.

Immaculate Conception The teaching that the Virgin Mary was so specially favoured by God that she was without sin from the moment she was conceived in her mother's womb. This teaching was defined as a doctrine of the Church by Pope Pius IX in 1854.

Immortality The quality of living forever. Jesus taught that those who believe in him and live according to his teachings will be raised from the dead and will live forever in happiness (John 11:25, 26).

Impediment to marriage Reasons or facts which, according to the laws of the Church, would prevent a couple from being married to each other.

Imprimatur Latin word meaning 'let it be printed'. An official permission given by a qualified Church authority for the printing of a book. The imprimatur declares that nothing in the book is against the teaching of the church.

Incarnation (Latin *incarnatio*, becoming flesh.) The central mystery of Christianity is that God took on human nature and became a man in the person of Jesus Christ.

Incense A mixture of gums and spices which, when burned, gives off a sweet perfume. The Jews used to burn incense during ceremonies and sacrifices in the Temple, as well as in daily life, to symbolise offering and worship, and to purify the air. Incense is sometimes used today in certain liturgical ceremonies. It is used far more frequently in the ceremonies of the Eastern churches. The smoke of burning incense symbolises the honour due to a person or sacred object in the liturgy. It is also a symbol of prayer and worship rising to God.

Indult (Latin *indultum*, a special favour.) Special permission given to someone by the Holy See to do something that is not normally allowed by Church law.

Infallibility Freedom from error; the quality of not making a mistake. The First Vatican Council (1870) teaches that the Pope cannot be in error when, as the supreme shepherd and teacher of the faithful, he proclaims some doctrine of faith or morals to be held by all the faithful. The Second Vatican Council also teaches that the bishops of the world cannot be in error when, in agreement with the Pope, they decree that a particular teaching, involving faith or morals, is to be held by all the members of the church. The particular teaching, in this case, must agree with what has been revealed in scripture and Christian tradition. The doctrine of infallibility is a way of saying that the Church is under the protection of the Holy Spirit, and so is free from error in matters concerning faith and morals.

Infancy narratives Stories in the gospels of Matthew and Luke telling of the birth and childhood of Jesus.

Initiation, Christian *See* Sacraments of initiation.

Inquisition A group of judges who were responsible for the trial and punishment of those who taught or followed false beliefs. People suspected of heresy were tortured by the Inquisition until they confessed their error. The Inquisition was set up in the thirteenth century under Pope Gregory IX. It no longer exists and is not something the Church is proud of.

INRI Abbreviation for the Latin *Iesus Nazarenus Rex Iudaeorum*, meaning Jesus of Nazareth, King of the Jews. Pilate had it written above Jesus as he hung on the cross. It was written in Hebrew, Greek and Latin, to explain to people that Jesus was crucified because he claimed to be a king.

Inspiration (Latin *inspirare*, breathe into.) The writers of the books in the Bible are said to be inspired by God. That means the ideas they wrote down were the very ideas and truths God wants us to know about, so that we might understand more about God, and be the kind of people God wants us to be. This does not mean that every word is inspired but that the religious ideas are inspired.

Intercession (Latin *intercessio*, a coming between.) Intercession occurs when people pray for others. When the saints plead with God for human beings here on earth, they offer prayers of intercession.

Intercommunion Intercommunion occurs when, under certain conditions, members of other Christian churches may receive Holy Communion at a celebration of the Eucharist in a Church to which they do not belong.

Introductory rites The rites at the beginning of Mass which come before the reading from scripture. The introductory rites consist of the entrance, the greeting, introductory remarks by the priest or commentator, the penitential rite, the Glory to God, the opening prayer.

Isaiah A prophet in Jerusalem, active between about 742–701 BCE. His name is similar in meaning to Jesus, 'Yahweh is salvation'.

Islam (Arabic *islam*, submission [to the will of God].) The religion of the Muslims, based on the teachings of Muhammad, which are found in the scriptures of Islam, the Koran. Muhammad (*c.* 570–632 CE) was an Arab prophet who converted his people from paganism to the worship of Allah. Islam (pronounced i-SLAHM) teaches that there is only one god, Allah, to whom all Muslims must submit themselves. It is the dominant religions in the Middle East, and its centre is the holy city of Mecca in Arabia. Islam is one of the largest and fastest growing religions in the world. The five pillars of Islam are: witness to the faith (there is no God but Allah), prayer (said five times a day), fasting, almsgiving, pilgrimage (once in a lifetime a Muslim is required to make a religious journey to Mecca).

Israel Name given to the patriarch Jacob in the story of his wrestling with the angel (Genesis 32:23–33). The name sounds like the Hebrew words for 'let God struggle'. It became the name for the 'children of Israel' (Israelites) and was used to describe the whole nation. When the northern kingdom broke away from the southern kingdom of Judah, it was called the kingdom of Israel. It is the official name of the modern Jewish state. *See also* Palestine.

Jacob Short form of Hebrew name Ya'aqubh–el (let God protect). Son of Isaac and Rebecca, twin brother of Esau, Jacob was the father of twelve sons who became the leaders of the twelve tribes of Israel.

Jacobite Church A Church founded in 543 CE by a monk, Jacob Baradai, who was made Bishop of Edessa in south-eastern Turkey. The Jacobites believe that Jesus was only partly divine and partly human. The Jacobite patriarch lives in Damascus, Syria, and rules over eleven dioceses: four in Syria, two in Iraq, two in Turkey, one in Lebanon, one in Jerusalem, and one in New Jersey, USA.

Jainism An Indian religion that broke away from Hinduism. The followers of Jainism do not believe in a supreme God.

Jehovah Another form of the name Yahweh. Both names are based on the Hebrew letters YHWH, which is the name of God.

Jehovah's Witnesses A religious group who believe that God will one day establish a new creation because our world is under the control of Satan. At that time Christ will defeat Satan and there will be a final judgement and only 144,000 people will be saved. The Witnesses do not believe in the Trinity or the divinity of Christ.

Jerusalem The city in the hills of Judea that was once inhabited by the Jebusites, who named it after the Canaanite god Shalem. It was captured by King David, who established it as the capital of the Jewish kingdom. Solomon built the Temple on the hill in Jerusalem where Abraham was believed to have come to offer his son Isaac. The city is at an altitude of over 700 metres and was watered in ancient times by the spring Gihon. The Romans destroyed Jerusalem and the Temple in 70 CE. Today, it is holy to the Jews because it is where the Temple once stood. It is holy to the Muslims because the prophet Muhammad ascended into heaven from Jerusalem, and it is holy to the Christians because Jesus spent some time there and was crucified just outside the city. *See also* Zion.

Jesuits Members of the Society of Jesus, a religious order of men founded by St Ignatius of Loyola in 1540. The Jesuits are noted for their solidarity with the Pope and their dedication to education and learning.

Jesus (Aramaic *yeshua*, Yahweh is salvation.) A name commonly given to Palestinian males in New Testament times. The Hebrew form of this name is Joshua. The early followers of Jesus added the title 'Christ', which means messiah, in order to express their belief that Jesus is the Messiah.

Jew (Hebrew *yehudi*, member of the tribe of Judah.) Word used to describe the people of Israel. It was commonly used after the fall of the northern kingdom of Israel in 721 BCE to describe the ethnic race of people living in the Persian province of Judah. A person is considered to be Jewish by birth if her/his mother is Jewish. The Second Vatican Council encourages understanding and deep fellowship between Jews and Christians.

Jewish Council *See* Sanhedrin

Jubilee year The book of Leviticus (25:10) declares that every fiftieth year should be a jubilee year. In Jewish tradition all debts were written off, slaves were freed and all property had to be returned to its original owner. These old customs are no longer practised in Judaism.

Judaism The religion of the Jewish people based on the laws and traditions of the Hebrew scriptures and the teaching of the rabbis found in the Talmud. Jews believe in the one and only God who created all things and who is the source of all goodness.

Judgement The Israelites regarded God as the one who would judge all people according to the good they have done. They believed God would reward or punish people with long life and prosperity. Christian writers of the New Testament looked forward to a time when Jesus would come to judge all the world, and would reward the good people with everlasting happiness. The Church teaches that the particular judgement of a person takes place at the moment of death. The general judgement of all people will take place at Christ's second coming on the last day.

Julian calendar The calendar, set up by Julius Caesar in 46 BCE, consisting of a year of 365 days and a leap year (366 days) every four years. It is followed today by the Ukranian and Russian Catholic Church and the Orthodox churches. The Julian calendar was replaced by the Gregorian calendar in western Europe in the sixteenth century because it was inaccurate by ten days. *See also* Calendar.

Jurisdiction (Latin *iurisdictio*, administration of the law, authority.) This word refers to the church's power to make laws, to administer them and to pass sentence and make judgements in Church matters that deal with the well-being of the Church's members.

Justice (Latin *iustitia*, right.) In the Hebrew scriptures, justice is a virtue by which people carry out the demands of a relationship, whether it is with God or with other people. These demands differed, depending on the nature of the relationship. In the New Testament, faith in Jesus Christ puts the Christian in a special relationship with him. The 'just' believers will honour this relationship in the way they live. Through justice, people respect the rights of other individuals and groups, e.g. the right to a decent standard of living, the right to be educated, the right to live in peace and freedom.

Kingdom of God The reign of God over all people. The biblical idea was that people had to accept God as their king in order to be part of the kingdom of God. The kingdom or reign of God happens wherever people live in harmony with the will of God. It can be in our hearts, in our families and our world. Jesus proclaimed the kingdom of God, and said that we are already in the kingdom if we live the Christian life. We will live more completely in the kingdom after our death.

Knowledge (Greek *gnosis*, knowledge.) Knowing facts or persons. The Hebrew people gained knowledge through experience, so they knew with the heart. To know somebody was to have a relationship with that person. In the New Testament, to know Jesus is to experience him and have a loving relationship with him.

Koran (Arabic *qur'an*, a reading or recitation.) The sacred writings of Islam. The Koran (sometimes written Qur'an) contains the teachings of the prophet Muhammad. Muslims believe these teachings are revelations from God, passed on to Muhammad by the angel Gabriel. *See also* Islam.

Laity (Greek *laos*, people.) The laity share in the mission of the Church because of their union with Jesus Christ through baptism. This word is commonly used to describe the people of God who have not been ordained deacon, priest or bishop.

Lamb of God Jesus is called the Lamb of God because he sacrificed himself as a victim on the cross. The lamb was commonly used as a victim on the altar in the days when the Jews offered animal sacrifices to God. *See also* Agnus Dei.

L'Arche A French word meaning ark, Noah's ark. It is the name of a worldwide community of people, many of whom have disabilities, who come from different religions, languages and races. L'Arche is based on the idea that people with disabilities have the same dignity as everyone else. Members of L'Arche that do not have disabilities give practical help and support to those who do. L'Arche was founded in France in 1964 by the Canadian Jean Vanier and, like Noah's ark, is a place of refuge and protection for all kinds of people.

Last days The final days when the world will come to an end and Jesus Christ will come for the second time. Following this, there will be a general judgement of all the human race.

Last Supper The last meal Jesus ate with his followers. At this special meal Jesus gave himself to his disciples in the sacrament of the Eucharist and asked his disciples to remember him every time they gathered to eat their community meal. The early Christians called this sacred meal the Lord's Supper. *See also* Eucharist.

Latin The language spoken in the ancient Italian province of Latium. It later became the official language of the Roman Empire in the West and the Catholic Church centred on Rome.

Latin rite *See* Roman rite.

Law A rule or a collection of rules designed to keep order among people and protect their rights. In the Bible the tribes of Israel were regulated by tribal laws and customs. These were unified and organised under Moses (*see* Torah). The law of Christ is summed up in the law of love of God, ourselves and other people.

Lay ministers of Holy Communion Lay people who are specially appointed to distribute Holy Communion at Mass, and to take Communion to the sick.

Lay ministries The activities of lay people, as individuals or as organisations, who care for others in a variety of ways. Lay ministries include liturgical ministries, e.g. lectors, ministers of Communion; teaching ministries, e.g. teachers, catechists; pastoral ministries, e.g. care of the sick, counselling people in difficulties. The main duty of Christian men and women is to show, by the way they live and care for others, that they are followers of Jesus Christ.

Lectern A reading stand in church from which the readings from scripture are proclaimed during the Liturgy of the Word. *See also* Ambo.

Lectionary (Latin *lectionarium*, a book of readings.) The book containing the readings from scripture that are to be read at Mass on weekdays, Sundays, feasts and special Masses throughout the liturgical year.

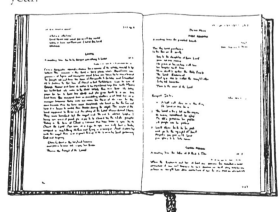

Lectionary

Lector A lay person who has the special task of reading the first and second readings in the Liturgy of the Word. Lectors have the important function of allowing the people to hear God speaking through the inspired scriptures.

Legion of Mary An association of lay people dedicated to assisting the Church in caring for people. It was founded in Dublin in 1921.

Lent The Old English word for spring. The period of forty days from Ash Wednesday to Holy Saturday. It is a time of penance when people are asked to fast and prepare for the commemoration of the sufferings, death and resurrection of Jesus. In the Eastern Catholic rites, Lent is a fifty-day period of penance known as the Great Fast.

Levite Member of the Jewish priestly tribe of Levi. Levites were not priests but assisted the priests in the Temple and shrines. They also acted as Temple guards. Most of them, especially those from the country, were quite poor.

Liberation Theology A way of thinking about God and Christianity that seeks to make changes in the world that will put an end to oppression and disadvantage. Liberation theologians believe that God intended people to live in a world where everyone is given respect and justice. They point out the evils in poverty, sexism, racism and the power that some people have over others.

Life everlasting The Hebrews believed God was the author of all life. They did not think about life after death until later in their development as a religious people. Even in the time of Jesus opinion was divided. The Pharisees believed in a personal resurrection after death while the Sadducees did not. The New Testament writers believed in a personal resurrection, after which we will live in the happiness of God's life and love. Jesus himself rose from the dead and promised life everlasting to those who followed him and remained faithful to the law of love.

Litany (Greek *litaneia*, prayer.) A prayer consisting of many short titles and requests, which are followed by responses.

Liturgical colours Colours used for vestments and cloths which decorate churches. The colours symbolise the spirit of a feast or season, e.g. white is for joy and is used at such festivals as Christmas and Easter; violet or purple is for penance and sorrow and is used in the seasons of Advent and Lent.

Liturgical year An arrangement of the year according to Church seasons in which events of the life of Christ are recalled. For example, the Christmas season recalls and celebrates the birth of Christ, Easter recalls the resurrection.

Liturgy (Greek *leitourgia*, public service, public worship.) (1) The collection of actions, songs and words that expresses the relationship between God and the people when they are assembled for worship, and between the members of the community themselves. (2) The actions, songs and words that make up the prayers and ceremonies of the Mass or eucharistic worship. The different parts of the liturgy come together as a unified whole making it an act of thanksgiving and joy which comes from a celebrating community. (3) The official prayer of the Church for special times of the day.

Liturgy of the Eucharist The part of the Mass that begins with the preparation of the gifts, and ends with the prayer after Communion. In the Liturgy of the Eucharist the gifts are prepared, Jesus' work of redemption is recalled, and God is thanked for giving Jesus Christ to the world.

Liturgy of the Hours Prayer of the Church that takes place at important times of the day. The idea comes from ancient Jewish tradition in which prayer was offered to God during the day. In the Western Church these 'sacred times' are morning, midmorning, midday, midafternoon, evening and night. Prayer is offered at these times with the recitation of psalms and readings from scripture. In monastic orders the monks and nuns have always gathered at these times to sing the Office or Liturgy of the Hours.

Liturgy of the Word The part of the Mass that begins with first scriptural reading and ends after the prayer of the faithful. The readings are taken from the Hebrew scriptures and the New Testament. The first reading is followed by the singing or recitation of a psalm (this is the responsorial psalm) and the second reading is followed by the alleluia or gospel acclamation, which prepares for the reading of the gospel.

Lord In the Bible, 'Lord' is a Hebrew title for God, for the king and for a husband. Adonai was the usual way of referring to Yahweh as Lord. The earliest Christians confessed their faith by saying 'Jesus is Lord'. This was a way of recognising that God had glorified Jesus after his resurrection, and that Jesus was with God in glory.

Lord's Day Sunday is called the Lord's Day because it is a day set aside for offering prayer and worship to the Lord. The first Christians gathered to celebrate the resurrection of Jesus Christ on Sunday and this is why we worship and take part in the Eucharist on this day. *See also* Sunday.

Lord's Prayer The 'Our Father', which is the prayer that Jesus taught his followers to pray (Matthew 6:9–13).

Lord's Supper The Last Supper of Jesus and his disciples. The early Christians always called their eucharistic meals the Lord's Supper.

Lord's table The altar used at Mass.

Lourdes A small town in southern France where a peasant girl, Bernadette Soubirous, is said to have had repeated visions of Our Lady in 1858. It is now a major place of pilgrimage where many people claim to have been cured of illness and disabilities. *See also* Apparition.

Love Strong liking for someone else. The relationship between God and us is one of love. When people are truly loving they come closer to God. We can lead a full Christian life by loving God and other people. Two Greek words are used in the New Testament for love: (1) *philia*, a word which describes a warm, close friendship or real affection; (2) *agape*, which is the most common New Testament word for love, refers to the will and not to emotions. True Christian love or *agape* comes from a decision to live the kind of life that tries to bring about the good of other people (1 Corinthians 13:1–13).

Loving-kindness Used to translate the Hebrew word *hesed* (faithfulness, loyalty). It generally refers to God's continual loyalty and abiding love for humanity.

Lutheran A member of the Protestant Church founded by Martin Luther (1483–1546) in the sixteenth century. The Lutheran Church is strong in Germany and Scandinavia.

Madonna Italian word meaning 'my lady'. It is a title given to Mary, and is used mainly of paintings and statues representing her.

Magi Priests of the Zoroastrian religion in ancient Persia who practised magic and studied the stars. The Magi in Matthew's Gospel (2:1–12) could have come from Persia, Arabia or Mesopotamia.

Magisterium (Latin *magister,* master, teacher.) The teaching authority of the church. The Pope and bishops have this authority by reason of their position in the Church.

Magnificat *See* Canticle of Mary.

Malabar rite The Syro-Malabar rite is the liturgy used by the Eastern Catholics of Malabar in southern India. The Syriac language and much of the Syriac liturgy are used, although there are many practices that are like those of the Roman Catholic Church.

Manger Box or trough containing cattle feed, such as hay or straw. After he was born, Jesus was laid in a manger because his parents could not afford to place him in a proper cradle.

Manna A sweet substance given off by certain insects and left on the stalks and leaves of trees. It dries as a whitish or yellowish sticky lump. God provided manna in the desert as food for the Israelites (Exodus 16).

Maranatha An expression in the language spoken by Jesus (Aramaic), which means 'Our Lord, come!' It was used by the early Christians at a time when they believed that Jesus would return to earth quite soon.

Marian devotions Prayers and practices that honour the Blessed Virgin Mary. As the mother of Jesus and the mother of all Christians, Mary asks her son for the peace and happiness of all people. In Catholic tradition the months of May and October are times of special devotion to Mary.

Maronites Members of the Arabic-speaking Eastern Catholic rite (Maronite Rite), which is centred in Lebanon. They take their name from St Maron (died 433 CE), a famous abbot and ascetic who lived in Lebanon. He is regarded as their Patriarch or founder. In Australia there are many Maronite Catholics. Their archbishop lives in Sydney and they have parishes around Australia.

Marriage (Latin *maritare,* unite.) A commitment made by a man and a woman that they will be united as husband and wife in a union that is permanent, exclusive and open to the possibility of children. When they get married Catholics speak of the sacrament of Marriage or Matrimony because they believe that this union is a mysterious reflection of the shared love between Christ and his Church. This sacrament enables them to help each other grow in love, to bring up their children in a happy Christian family, and to show by their life together that God's love is alive in them and in their children.

Marriage tribunal A Church court to which Catholics go when they want to have their marriage annulled (*see* Annulment). Non-Catholics who have already been married and who then wish to marry a Catholic or become a Catholic and marry in the Catholic Church, also go there to have their former marriage investigated confidentially. The tribunal is made up of people who investigate marriage to see if there are good reasons for an annulment to be granted.

Martyrology List of the early Church martyrs with short stories of their lives.

Martyrs (Greek *martyr,* witness.) People who give witness to their faith by willingly suffering death rather than give up their religious beliefs.

Mary The mother of Jesus who is the Son of God. Mary was chosen by God to be the mother of the saviour and was preserved from all sin from the moment of her conception. In Catholic tradition Mary was a virgin before and after the birth of her son. Mary and her husband, Joseph, raised Jesus in the Galilean village of Nazareth.

Mass (Latin *missa,* dismissal.) The celebration of the Eucharist. The name comes from the Latin words *ite missa est,* which were formerly used for the dismissal at the end of the liturgy.

Materialism An idea that there is nothing more to life than what we can pick up with our senses. Materialists do not believe in spiritual things. In everyday speech a 'materialist' is one who has no spiritual life but who thinks the gaining of money and possessions is the most important thing in life.

Matrimony (Latin *matrimonium,* marriage.) The sacrament of Marriage.

Maundy Thursday Thursday in Holy Week. Maundy comes from the Latin *mandatum* (commandment), which recalls John 13:34: 'A new commandment I give to you …' In the days before Vatican II, when the liturgy was in Latin, the antiphon for the ceremony of the Washing of the Feet began with the words *mandatum novum. See also* Holy Thursday.

Meditation Reflecting on and thinking over the things that involve God and God's relationship with humanity. It can be thinking over the events and experiences contained in the Bible, e.g. the life of Jesus, or paying attention to God and being conscious of the presence of God. Silence and relaxation of mind and body are necessary for meditation.

Melkites (Melchites) Arabic-speaking Catholics of Syria, Egypt and the Holy Land. They are called Melkites from the Hebrew word *melek* which means king. The Melkite rite is part of the Byzantine rite and is conducted in Arabic. In the early centuries of Christianity the Melkites remained faithful to Church teachings as proclaimed by the king or emperor in Constantinople. There are many Melkite Catholics in Australia. Their bishop lives in Sydney and they have parishes around the country.

Memorare Prayer to the Blessed Virgin composed by St Bernard of Clairvaux (1090–1153). Its title is the first word of the Latin version. The prayer asks the Blessed Virgin for help, and reminds her that she has never let anybody down.

Mercy Help given to people who need help. God showed mercy in saving the people of Israel and giving them life, forgiveness and prosperity. In the gospels, Jesus shows mercy by giving help to those who ask.

Mercy killing *See* Euthanasia.

Messenger One who is sent with a message. The Hebrew word may describe a prophet who is sent by God. The Greek word *angelos* means 'messenger'. Apostles were messengers who were sent by Jesus to spread the good news.

Messiah Hebrew word meaning 'anointed one'. The idea comes from Judaism which believed that God would one day send someone to overcome evil and set up the reign of God in the world. Christians believe that Jesus Christ has done this and is therefore the Messiah. *See also* Christ.

Metanoia Greek word meaning 'change of heart', 'turning away from sin towards God'. When people are sorry for sin they turn away from doing wrong and undergo a metanoia.

Metropolitan (1) The archbishop of a diocese which usually takes in the chief city of a larger province, state or territory that is divided into other dioceses with their own bishops. (2) The next highest rank to patriarch in the Eastern Orthodox Church.

Minister (Latin *minister,* servant, helper.) (1) A person ordained to preside at religious worship and care for the spiritual good of others. (2) A person with authority to minister or care for others.

Minister of the Eucharist The minister of the celebration of the Eucharist is the bishop or priest. The term 'Special Minister of the Eucharist' is sometimes used of lay people who assist with the distribution of Holy Communion. *See also* Acolyte *and* Lay ministers of Holy Communion.

Minister of the Word The Apostles were first called the ministers of the word (Acts 6:4) because they spoke about Jesus and his teaching. Today's ministers of the word are those who communicate the teachings of scripture to the people of God. Ordained ministers also have the task of passing on the message of Christ through the preaching of the word and the celebration of the sacraments.

Ministry The use of a person's gifts, talents and energy for the service of others. All people have different gifts in the Church and are called to serve others in their own way.

Miracle (Latin *miraculum,* a wonder.) An event in which we can see an act or revelation of God. One of the Greek words for miracle is *dynamis* (from which we get dynamite). The miracles are works of power. In John's gospel they are called signs because they point beyond themselves. The miracles are signs of God acting in history.

Missal A book containing the formulas and rights for the celebration of the Eucharist. It contains the prayers said by the priest at different kinds of Masses throughout the year as well as the responses made by the people.

Mission (Latin *missio,* a sending.) (1) The mission of the Church, which involves all its members, is the task of spreading the good news of salvation through Jesus Christ, of serving others and of building up the Christian community. (2) A group of people (missionaries) sent to a foreign land for the religious conversion of the inhabitants. (3) The territory in which missionaries work for the spread of the kingdom of God.

Mitre (Greek *mitra,* headdress.) Ceremonial headdress worn by a bishop as a sign of office in liturgical functions.

Mixed marriage Marriage between a Catholic and a baptised non-Catholic. The Catholic partner in a mixed marriage agrees to do everything in his/her power to see that any children of the marriage are baptised as Catholics and grow in the Catholic faith.

Modernism A movement which claimed that the church's teachings ought to be presented in a way that fitted in with the philosophy and science of the late nineteenth and early twentieth centuries. It was condemned by Pope Pius X, in 1907, because it appeared to attack the permanence of Church teaching.

Monastery (Greek *monasterion,* solitary dwelling.) A house or residence occupied by a community of monks who are dedicated to a life of prayer and service.

Monasticism A way of life followed by men and women dedicated to a particular religious life in monasteries. Christian monasticism began around the third century CE and grew out of the practice of Christians who went into remote places to spend their time in prayer and simple works. Western monasticism began to flourish after the time of St Benedict (around 480–540). By the Middle Ages there were many monasteries all over Europe and they became well-known centres of learning and culture.

Monk (Greek *monachos,* lone, solitary.) A man who has given up living in a town or in the country and goes to a monastery where he can live an ordered life of prayer, contemplation and work for the sake of the Gospel. Monks take vows of poverty, chastity and obedience, and usually live together in communities. They also take a fourth vow of stability, that is, to remain in one monastery.

Mitre

Monotheism (Greek *monos*, one; *theos*, god.) The belief that there is only one God and one God alone should be worshipped. The three major monotheistic religions are Judaism, Christianity and Islam.

Monsignor A title of honour given to certain priests who are not bishops.

Monstrance (Latin *monstrare,* to show.) A vessel used for displaying the sacred host of the Blessed Sacrament for adoration by the people.

Monstrance

Montanism A heresy begun by Montanus (about 156 CE), who said that sins could not be forgiven through the church. Montanism lasted about two hundred years.

Morality Living according to the rules of good behaviour. Christians try to live good lives because they are on their way to God, who is goodness itself. Those who follow the teachings of Jesus Christ will always try to do what is right and will love and respect God, themselves and other people. The scriptures, the teachings of the Church and each person's conscience help people understand what is right and wrong, and with the help of God's grace they choose to lead good, moral lives.

Mosque A Muslim house of prayer.

Mother of God This is Mary's greatest title and was officially proclaimed at the Council of Ephesus in 431. The title means that Mary is the mother of Jesus Christ, who is true God and true man.

Muslim *See* Islam.

Mystery (Greek *mysterion,* secret rite.) (1) A scene or event connected with the life of Christ. (2) Something which is too deep and rich for the human mind to understand. God is a mystery, but God is always being revealed in other people and in the natural world around us. In the New Testament, Christian teachings that were revealed only to those who had been baptised, were called sacred mysteries.

Mystics People who come to know more of God and other mysteries through personal religious experience and prayer. Mystical experience is open to everyone because it is an experience of grace. St Teresa of Avila and St John of the Cross were outstanding mystics.

Myth (Greek *mythos,* story.) A story about gods or superhuman beings usually told to try and explain the beginnings of social customs or things in nature. In the Bible there are myths that contain deeper truths about God's dealings with human beings. These myths are not like fairy stories but are stories that express the values and truths held by Jews and Christians. Myths are usually about things that cannot be understood, e.g. how the world came to be, what happens after death, and so are often imaginative stories that help humans understand the world and their place in it as well as their relationship with God.

Nativity (Latin *nativitas*, birth.) (1) The birth of Christ. (2) The Christian feast commemorating the birth of Christ, Christmas. (3) A picture or scene representing the birth of Christ.

Nazarene A person living in or from the town of Nazareth. Jesus was called a Nazarene (also Nazorean) because he lived there before he began his public life. The early Christians were called Nazoreans as an insult (Acts 24:5).

Neighbour An Israelite regarded only a fellow Israelite as a neighbour. Jesus said that our neighbour is any other human being.

Nestorianism A heresy named after Nestorius, bishop of Constantinople (428–431), who taught that the human Jesus and the divine Christ were actually two persons. He denied that Mary was the Mother of God and was condemned by the Council of Ephesus in 431.

New Age Spirituality A free-flowing spiritual movement of people who believe that everything that exists comes from a single source of divine energy. This movement became popular in the 1970s after many people thought that the major world religions had failed. New Age believers seek to establish a new age in which people are at peace and at one with themselves, each other and the whole universe.

New Testament Those books in the Bible that were written by the early Christians under the inspiration of God. The New Testament tells the story of Jesus and expresses the belief that Jesus was the Messiah promised in the Old Testament, and that he died and rose from the dead to save us from evil. The experiences of the early followers of Jesus are also described in the New Testament. The letters of Paul are the oldest New Testament documents and the gospels were written between about 70 and 100 CE. The last of the New Testament books, 2 Peter, was written around the middle of the second century.

Nicea, Council of (325 CE**)** The first universal (ecumenical) council. Emperor Constantine called the council hoping to bring about the unity of the Church through an agreement over the teaching about the relationship between Christ and God the Father. The council decreed that God the Father and the Son Jesus are one in being but separate in person. The Son is therefore co-eternal with the Father and not a creature.

Nicene Creed A summary of Christian teachings drawn up by the bishops at the Council of Constantinople (381 CE). The bishops took the creed of the Council of Nicea and made additions to it. It is this creed that Catholics recite when they express their faith at Mass on Sunday. Its full name is the Niceno-Constantinopolitan Creed.

Novena (Latin *novenus*, nine each.) A period of prayer spanning nine days, either nine consecutive days or one day a week for nine weeks.

Novice (Latin *novus*, new.) A person who is training to become a full member of a religious order.

Novitiate The preparation period and the place of training for novices.

Nun (Latin *nonna*, originally an old woman, later a term of respect for an unmarried woman.) A woman who has taken vows of poverty, chastity and obedience, and lives in a community leading a life of prayer and work as a member of a religious order such as the Benedictines or Carmelites.

Nuptial Mass and blessing (Latin *nuptiae*, wedding.) A special Mass and blessing used at weddings. If the wedding ceremony is not part of the Mass then the nuptial blessing is given to the couple.

Octave (Latin *octava,* eighth.) The eight days made up of a feast day and the seven days following.

Old Testament The books of the Old Testament, or Hebrew scriptures, were all written before the time of Christ by people who were inspired by God. In these writings we find revelations about God to the people of Israel and the continuing promise to care for them and send a Messiah to save them from the power of evil. Christians believe that Jesus Christ was the promised Messiah. It is preferable, in modern times, not to use the term Old Testament but to refer to the Hebrew Scriptures or the First Testament.

Oral tradition (Latin *tradere,* hand on.) Stories of the culture of a society passed on by word of mouth from one generation to the next. A lot of what God reveals to people has been handed on by word of mouth. Some of this oral tradition has also been written down. *See* Matthew 15:2–6; 2 Thessalonians 2:15.

Ordain (Latin *ordinare,* appoint.) To consecrate a member of the community for the service of the Church through the sacrament of Holy Orders.

Orders *See* Holy Orders.

Ordinary, local (Vicars Apostolic) An official in the Church who is responsible for teaching, governing, administering the sacraments and exercising authority. For example, the Pope, all diocesan bishops, vicars, abbots and their deputies are ordinaries.

Ordinary time The period of the liturgical year that falls outside the seasons of Advent, Christmas, Lent and Easter.

Ordination The sacramental celebration of the giving of Holy Orders. In the ceremony the bishop places his hands on the candidate and prays that the Holy Spirit will give him the necessary spiritual gifts for carrying out his ministry of serving the Catholic community. Bishops, priests and deacons are the ordained ministers of the church.

Original sin A term that describes the situation now shared by all human beings. In this situation they will always have two tendencies: (1) to do good and (2) to turn away from God and do evil. The Bible story shows that so many of the problems in our world come from the selfishness and greed of people who do not put God first in their lives. Jesus Christ came on earth to redeem human nature by his life, message, death and resurrection, and to show people how they can overcome their original sinfulness with the help of God's free gift of grace.

Orthodox (Greek *orthodoxos,* right teaching or opinion.) (1) The orthodox Christian is the one who is faithful to the Church's belief in Jesus Christ as expressed in the Bible, liturgy, Church teaching and daily living. (2) Reference to the Eastern churches not in union with Rome, e.g. the Greek Orthodox Church.

Orthodox churches Those churches in the East that have been faithful to the teachings of the Council of the Chalcedon (451 CE), but which refused to acknowledge the authority of the Pope, and have been separated from the Roman Catholic Church since the eleventh century, e.g. the Greek Orthodox Church.

Our Father *See* Lord's Prayer.

Pagan (Latin *paganus,* peasant, civilian.) People who were not Christians were called pagans by the early followers of Christ, because they were not 'soldiers' of Christ.

Palestine The name comes from the Philistines, who occupied the coastal area of the country a thousand years before the time of Christ. Palestine lay between the Jordan River (east) and the Mediterranean Sea (west), and between Mount Hermon (north) and the Negev Desert (south).

Palm Sunday The Sunday before Easter, now called Passion Sunday. On this day palm leaves are blessed and carried in procession to recall the time when Christ entered Jerusalem and the people called him a king.

Papal States Land and towns in Italy given to the Pope in 756 CE by Peptone, king of the Franks. These states were organised by Charlemagne in 800 CE. In 1870 the Pope lost control of the Papal States and his civil authority was limited to the Vatican City.

Papyrus (Greek *papyros,* papyrus plant.) A reed plant that grew in ancient Egypt. Strips of fibre from this plant were joined in vertical and horizontal rows to form a surface for writing. The English word 'paper' comes from papyrus.

Parable (Greek *parabole,* comparison, wise saying.) A saying or story used to illustrate a teaching. More than half of Jesus' teaching was done through parables. In these stories the main idea was that God and the kingdom of God can be seen in the lives of ordinary people.

Paraclete (Greek *parakletos,* helper, advocate.) In the New Testament, Jesus is called a paraclete who speaks for us to the Father (1 John 2:1). Jesus also promised to send the Spirit to his disciples as a helper. When Christians today speak of the Holy Paraclete, they generally mean the Holy Spirit, who takes the life, love and truth of Christ and makes them present in the hearts of people.

Paradise From a Persian word meaning a garden with trees and grass, and a stream running through it. It is another name for heaven.

Paraliturgy A communal act of devotion or a prayer service that is not strictly a part of the liturgy. A paraliturgy will usually consist of readings from scripture and other sources, together with songs and prayers.

Parish (Greek *paroikia,* neighbourhood.) A district that has its own church and clergyman. A diocese is made up of a number of parishes.

Parish council A group in the parish elected or appointed to help advise the parish priest and assist with all aspects of parish life.

Parish priest The priest in charge of a parish.

Parishioner A member of a parish.

Parousia (Greek *parousia,* presence, arrival.) The second coming of Christ at the end of the world.

Pasch (Greek *pascha,* coined from the Hebrew word *pesach* Passover.) The Jewish feast of Passover. *See also* Passover.

Paschal candle The large candle blessed at the beginning of the Easter Vigil. Inserted into the candle in the form of a cross, are five grains of incense, which represent the five wounds of Jesus. The candle and its light represent Christ, who is the light of the world, showing us the way to God.

Paschal candle

Paschal lamb The lamb which was sacrificed on the eve of the Jewish feast of Passover. Jesus Christ is compared to the paschal lamb because he was the victim offered in the sacrifice of the cross.

Paschal Mystery This refers to what God has done for humanity through the death of Jesus Christ. Jesus is like the Jewish Passover because he enabled people to pass from the slavery of sin to freedom.

Passion (Latin *passio,* suffering.) The suffering of Jesus during the last two days of his life. Each of the gospels has a passion story, or passion narrative, which describes the events of Jesus' suffering and death.

Passion Sunday *See* Palm Sunday.

Passover (Hebrew *pesach,* passing over.) The chief festival of Judaism, which celebrates the delivery of the Israelites from slavery in Egypt (Exodus 12:21–28). At Passover, Jewish families eat a meal of roast lamb and recall the events of the Exodus. In the New Testament the Last Supper of Jesus is linked with Passover.

Pastor (Latin *pastor,* shepherd.) A person (e.g. the parish priest) who cares for the spiritual life of a group of people.

Pastoral letter (1) A letter written by the bishop of a diocese to all the priests and people of the diocese. These letters may be read out by the priest to the people at Mass, or the bishop may read his letter onto a cassette tape which is played in the church on Sunday. (2) Letter in the New Testament written to individual community leaders (e.g. Timothy, Titus) to advise them how to organise the Christian community.

Paten (Latin *paterna*, dish.) A dish, shaped like a saucer, that holds the host at Mass. It is placed on top of the chalice.

Pater Noster Latin words meaning 'Our Father'.

Patriarch (1) An ancestor or father of the Israelite nation, mentioned in the Bible from Abraham to Joseph. (2) In the Eastern Catholic churches a patriarch is subject only to the Pope, and is head of all those who belong to his Church throughout the world.

Patron saint A saint who has special care for a country, a city, a group or a person who has the same name as the saint. Special prayers are offered to the patron saint by such people.

Peace (Latin *pax,* peace, tranquillity of mind.) The Israelites greeted each other with the wish for peace and wholeness (*shalom*). To wish people peace means to wish that they will enjoy harmony, prosperity, wholeness and calm in their lives. Conversion to Christianity, in the New Testament, put a person at peace with God. Christians used the Hebrew greeting of 'peace be with you' when they met each other. *See also* Sign of peace.

Penance (Latin *poenitentia,* regret.) (1) An act of prayer or self-denial carried out by a person as part of his/her sorrow for sin and decision to turn to God and away from evil. Catholics traditionally undertake penance especially in Lent. (2) Official name of one of the seven sacraments. In the sacrament of Penance there are various rites of Reconciliation.

Penitent A person who is sorry for sin and asks for reconciliation.

Penitential rite The first part of the Mass in which we say to God and to all the people present that we are sorry for our sins, and we ask for forgiveness. This prepares us to take part in the Eucharist.

Penitential season Lent is the chief penitential season of the liturgical year, when people pray and perform acts of self-denial to say they are sorry for their sins and to prepare for the festival of Easter.

Pentateuch (Greek *pente* five; *teuchos* volume.) The first five books of the Hebrew Bible: Genesis, Exodus, Leviticus, Numbers, Deuteronomy. The Pentateuch holds pride of place in the Hebrew tradition, where it is generally known as Torah.

Pentecost (Greek *pentekoste,* fiftieth.) Israelite-Jewish festival of weeks occurring fifty days after Passover. It originally marked the end of the wheat harvest. It also commemorated the day God gave the law to Moses. In Christian tradition it marks the coming of the Spirit to the followers of Jesus (Acts 2:5). This enabled them to go out and spread the good news about Jesus. Pentecost is the conclusion of the Easter season.

Pentecostal movement A movement based on the idea that people have direct contact with the Holy Spirit in prayer groups and other activities. These people are said to have charismatic experiences (e.g. the gift of tongues, prophecy, healing). The Holy Father has said there are three ways in which people can judge whether something is truly from the Spirit: (1) it agrees with the teaching of the church; (2) it helps others; and (3) it encourages love among the people.

People of God In the Hebrew scriptures the Israelites are specially chosen people of God. Early Christians regarded themselves as the new Israel, the true people of God. The idea that the Church is the people of God reminds Christians that they are members of God's community, and do not go to God on their own.

Permanent deacon A position that was re-established in the Church by Pope Paul VI in 1967, allowing males (who may be married or unmarried) to be ordained deacons to assist the parish clergy. They receive some instruction, but not the same training as priests, and perform functions such as preaching, presiding over weddings, burials, baptisms.

Persecution Deliberate attempt by some people to make individuals or a group suffer for their beliefs. Generally the persecutors try to force the believers to give up their faith or die. The Jewish people have a history of being persecuted by foreigners. Christians were persecuted by Roman authorities in the second and third centuries. Even today some countries are persecuted for their religion, e.g. Poland, Russia, parts of South America.

Petition (Latin *petitio,* request.) A request made for something we desire. A prayer of petition is one in which we ask a favour from God.

Pew (Latin, *podium,* balcony.) A seat like bench used by the people in church.

Pharaoh (Egyptian *per'o,* great house.) A title given to the kings of ancient Egypt.

Pharisee (Hebrew *parash,* separate.) A group in Judaism who dedicated themselves to spiritual renewal and faithful observance of the law of Moses. The word 'Pharisee' means 'separate' in the way that someone holy is set apart or separated for the service of God. After the destruction of the Temple in 70 CE the Pharisees became the spiritual leaders of Judaism, and when the emerging Christian Church split away from Judaism Christians and Jews became rivals and even enemies. This bitterness is present in the gospels and can give the impression that Jesus was opposed to all Pharisees rather than to the excessive narrowness of some of them.

Pilgrim (Latin *peregrinus,* foreigner.) One who travels to a holy place in order to show devotion and gain some spiritual benefit.

Pilgrimage The journey made by a pilgrim to a shrine or place of devotion in order to pray and pay respect to the particular person venerated or buried at the holy place. Christians have always visited the Holy Land to make pilgrimage to the places connected with the life of Jesus. During the Middle Ages the pilgrimage was very popular as a form of penance for sin.

Plainchant Simple melodies in certain kinds of scales called modes were used for the singing of parts of the Mass and the Divine Office in the earliest days of the Church. This style of singing is called chant or plainchant or plainsong. *See* Gregorian chant.

Pontiff (Latin *pontifex,* bridge builder.) The bishop of Rome, the Pope. The ancient pagans believed that a priest who offered sacrifice was a go-between for humans and the god they worshipped. The title 'pontiff' was given to the Pope as the vicar or representative of Christ on earth.

Pontifical Mass Solemn Mass celebrated by a bishop. The liturgical book containing all rites celebrated by a bishop is the Pontifical.

Pope (Greek *pappas,* father.) The Bishop of Rome and the elected spiritual leader of the Roman Catholic Church. The Second Vatican Council stressed the fact that the Pope exercises his authority in consultation and collegiality with the bishops of the church.

Postulant (Latin *postulans,* asking.) Person preparing to be admitted into a religious order.

Prayer (1) An act in which we lift our minds and hearts to God. Prayer can take many forms, e.g. thinking about Jesus, his life and the things he said and did; looking at the world around us and thinking of God who made it all out of love; saying prayers; singing hymns and sacred songs. (2) A form of words used for praying, e.g. the Our Father is a prayer.

Prayer of the faithful Prayers for the needs of the whole Church and the local community which are offered by the people at Mass. The prayer of the faithful comes just after the profession of faith called the Nicene Creed.

Preface (Latin *praefatio,* a saying beforehand.) The prayer of praise and thanksgiving that introduces the Eucharistic Prayer at Mass. It ends with the acclamation, 'Holy, holy, holy Lord, God of power and might …' The preface often recalls the feast being celebrated or the liturgical season of the year and so acts as an introduction to the Eucharistic Prayer.

Prelate (Latin *praelatus,* one who is chosen above others.) A high-ranking person in the Church, such as a bishop, cardinal, patriarch.

Preparation of the gifts After the prayer of the faithful at Mass, the gifts that will become the Lord's body and blood are brought to the altar. The preparation of the gifts ends when the priest says the prayer over the gifts.

Presbyter (Greek *presbyteros,* older man.) The senior men in the first Christian communities were respected for their wisdom and their faith in Christ. They acted as advisers to the community. The leaders of the community also presided at the liturgy. The presbyters presided in the parish churches when the bishop could not be present.

Presbyterian The name of various Protestant churches that do not have bishops but are governed by elected groups of lay elders or presbyters. These churches follow a modified form of Calvinism. *See also* Calvinism.

Presbytery (1) The council of elders in the early Christian communities. (2) The house or building in which the parish priest lives.

Presentation The feast on which Catholics commemorate the occasion when Jesus was presented in the Temple by Joseph and Mary (Luke 2:22–38). The feast was also called Candlemas and is celebrated on 2 February.

Priest (Greek *presbyteros,* older man.) (1) In the Catholic Church priests are ordained to preach the Word, preside over the liturgy and the celebration of the sacraments, and care for the pastoral needs of the Christian community. Priests are ordained to the order of Presbyter. *See also* Presbyter. (2) Men who conducted sacrifices in the Israelite shrines to Yahweh. They inherited their office from father to son.

Priesthood of all the faithful By being baptised into Christ all Christians share in the priesthood of Christ who is priest, prophet and king. The people of God offer a sacrifice to God by their good lives, their service to each other and their faithfulness to Jesus Christ. All believers are called to ministry by baptism.

Prior   The head of certain religious communities, e.g. Carthusians, Dominicans.

Procession   An organised movement of the clergy and people from one place to another. Processions are usually accompanied by prayers, music and singing.

Profession of faith   A statement of belief made by Christians. The Apostles' Creed, the Nicene Creed, the Athanasian Creed are professions of faith.

Profession, religious   An act by which certain people dedicate themselves in a special way to God. During the ceremony of religious profession the candidates publicly make vows of poverty, chastity and obedience and become committed members of religious orders or congregations. Profession can be made for a certain time (temporary) or for life (perpetual).

Propagation of the Faith   The department of the Roman Curia officially called the Congregation for the Evangelisation of Peoples. It is commonly known as Propaganda Fide (Propagation of the Faith). It is responsible for the missionary work of the church.

Prophet   (Greek *prophetes,* one who speaks out.) Prophets believed they were called by God to speak out against the evils and injustices of their time. They acted as mouthpieces of God. Amos was a prophet in ancient Israel and John the Baptist was a more recent prophet. There have been modern prophets, too, who speak out for justice in our own time, e.g. Bishop Helda Camara, Mahatma Gandhi and the thousands of people who are not afraid to stand up and speak out for what is right.

Protestant   A member of one of the Christian churches that separated from the Catholic Church during the Reformation, or any other Christian group descended from them. Those who started the Protestant movement 'protested' against some of the beliefs and contemporary abuses in the Catholic Catholic Church.

Protestantism   The religious movement started by Luther, Calvin and other Reformers, who protested against the things they disagreed with in the Catholic Church in the sixteenth century.

Provincial   The head of a province or district of a religious community.

Psalm   (Greek *psallo,* I sing.) Hebrew religious song addressed to God as a prayer. There are 150 songs in the book of Psalms.

Psalter   A book containing a collection of psalms for liturgical or devotional use.

Publican   (Latin *publicanus,* private tax agent.) People mentioned in the gospels who collected taxes for the Romans. They were hated by their fellow Jews because they helped the Roman enemy.

Pulpit   (Latin *pulpitus,* stage.) A platform or raised stage in a church from which the priest gives his sermon. In modern churches the priest usually preaches from a lectern, which is not as high as a pulpit.

Purgatory   (Latin *purgare,* cleanse.) A state of existence in which those who have died are cleansed of imperfections and selfishness before being united with God. The teachings of the Church do not describe purgatory, but repentance for all the sins of our life, and a complete turning towards God in love, are stressed in the Church's understanding of purgatory.

Purificator (purifier)   A small linen cloth used during the Mass to dry and clean the chalice.

Pyx   A small metal container in which the Blessed Sacrament is carried to the sick.

Q Document Many biblical scholars believe there was a collection of sayings of Jesus that circulated among the earliest Christians. It was customary for disciples to collect the teachings or sayings of their teacher and it is reasonable to believe that Jesus' followers had such a document. German scholars named this supposed document the 'source' (in German *Quelle* or Q).

Quakers *See* Friends, Society of.

Qumran *See* Dead Sea Scrolls *and* Essenes.

Rabbi (Aramaic *rab,* master, teacher.) (1) The word rabbi means 'my master', and refers to a Jewish scholar and to one who explains the Jewish law. Jesus was sometimes called rabbi by his followers and others. (2) After the destruction of Jerusalem in 70 CE, the Pharisaic rabbis reorganised the Jewish religion and established the synagogue as the community meeting-place for prayer and the study of the scriptures. The rabbi became the main religious official of a synagogue, equivalent to a Christian minister of religion.

RCIA Rite of Christian Initiation of Adults. This describes a program of instruction and preparation leading up to the reception of adults into the Catholic Church. Like catechesis, it is a journey into faith for the adult convert.

Real presence The teaching of the Church which states that the crucified and risen Christ is present in a special way in the Eucharist. The Second Vatican Council teaches that Jesus Christ is really present in the community that assembles for worship, in the person of the minister who presides in his name, in the biblical word that is proclaimed, and in the consecrated bread and wine.

Recessional song The song sung at the end of Mass as the priest and his assistants leave the altar.

Reconcile (Latin *reconciliare,* bring back, restore.) To restore or heal a broken friendship. This involves a change of attitude and action. In the Bible it is always people, not God, who break the friendship between God and humans (2 Corinthians 5:18–21).

Reconciliation, sacrament of Another name for the sacrament of Penance, in which a person celebrates with a priest the fact that she/he is sorry for sin and is being reconciled with God. This is also called the rite of Reconciliation. There are three common forms of this rite. The first rite is individual reconciliation between a penitent and the priest. The second rite is the reconciliation of several people, which consists of readings and prayers of preparation celebrated as a community and followed by individual confession and absolution with a priest. The third rite consists of a ceremony in which the priest and people prepare for reconciliation with prayers and readings from scripture, and then this is followed by a general absolution which the priest gives to everybody at once.

Rector (Latin *rector,* ruler.) The priest in charge of a seminary, religious house or congregation. In some countries the word is used for the parish priest.

Redeemer (Latin *redemptor,* a person who pays off a debt for somebody else.) Jesus Christ is called the redeemer because he won back the kingdom of heaven for the sinful human race by freely giving himself up to death. This was a sign of his total dedication to the demands of his mission.

Redemption (Latin *redimere,* buy back.) (1) The action of God in saving the Hebrew people from their enemies or some disaster. (2) The action of the life, death and resurrection of Jesus, which 'buys us back' from sin into the grace of God. Redemption is a gift from God by which we have been saved from the power of evil.

Reformation The period of religious change that divided Christians in Europe during the sixteenth century. Martin Luther in Germany and John Calvin in Switzerland tried to reform the Catholic Church and correct abuses, such as the sale of relics and indulgences, and the misuse of Church power. The followers of Luther and Calvin were known as Protestants. The Catholic Church eventually reformed itself with the Council of Trent (1545–63).

Relic (Latin *reliquiae,* things left behind.) Portion of a saint's clothing or body that has been preserved and honoured by believers as an expression of faith in Jesus Christ and belief in eternal life.

Religion (Latin *religio,* fear of the gods.) (1) The combination of attitudes, emotions, rituals, beliefs and organisations by which humans try to express their relationship with God and the world around them. (2) An organisation of people who follow a special set of rules, beliefs and practices in their effort to carry out their duties to their god and other people, e.g. the Christian religion.

Religious (1) Anything concerned with religion or sacred rites. (2) A member of a religious order who has made vows.

Religious freedom The right of individuals and groups to practise their religion without persecution or interference from governments or state laws.

Religious order A community of people who take solemn vows and live according to the rule drawn up by their founder, e.g. Carmelites, Benedictines. Religious orders are also called Institutes of Consecrated Life and Societies of Apostolic Life.

Renaissance (French *naissance,* birth.) A time of great revival or re-birth in culture, art and literature in Europe during the fourteenth, fifteenth and sixteenth centuries. In this period there was renewed interest in the art and culture of the classical world of ancient Greece and Rome. There was also a re-birth in politics, society and religion with the result the human mind and human achievement became the centre of interest and less attention was paid to God and the place of religion in human life. Where the Middle Ages in Europe were dominated by religious concerns the Renaissance period was more concerned with human activity.

Repent (Latin *poenitere,* be sorry.) To turn to God and away from evil. This involves a change of mind and a change in the way we act. Baptism, confession of sins and a good life are the signs of repentance in the New Testament and in the Church today. *See also* Convert.

Requiem (Latin *requies,* rest.) It comes from the Latin phrase *requiem aeternam* (eternal rest), and refers to a Mass offered for the dead, at funerals and on All Souls' Day.

Responsorial psalm A psalm sung or read after the first reading at Mass or in other celebrations of prayer. Part of that psalm is repeated after every verse as a response by the people.

Resurrection To come back to life. Jesus died and rose from the dead and so won victory over evil and death. Those who believe in Jesus will also be raised from the dead, and will live forever.

Retreat A time when a person turns away from everyday activities in order to rest, pray and think in peace and quiet

Revelation (Latin *revelo,* I unveil, uncover.) Revelation takes place when God communicates with us and enables us to grow into the fullness of our own lives. God's revelation can be seen in other people, signs, events, dreams, visions, ideas, history and the world of nature. Jesus Christ, through his life, personality and message, has given us the best revelation of God. Revelation takes place in the scriptures and in the community of the Church where we can learn a lot about God.

Reverend A title of respect given to a member of the clergy or a religious order, e.g. Reverend Father.

Rite (Latin *ritus,* ceremony.) (1) The religious and liturgical customs of a group of people who have their own priesthood and hierarchy, their own liturgical rules and canon law, and their own spiritual tradition. The principal rites are: Latin or Roman; Byzantine, including Bulgarian, Greek, Georgian, Italo-Albanian, Melkite, Romanian, Russian, Serbian, Ukrainian; Armenian, Catholic and Orthodox; Chaldean, including the Chaldean Catholics in Iraq and the Nestorian Christians; Alexandrian, including Coptic and Ethiopian; Malabar; Antiochene, including the Malankarese, Maronite and Orthodox Jacobite churches. (2) A single ceremony with its own special form, e.g. the rite of baptism.

Ritual (Latin *ritualis,* relating to religious ceremonies.) (1) Any action or set of actions symbolising the feelings or relationships that people have towards each other and the world around them. For example, shaking hands is a ritual that symbolises friendship or recognition. (2) An established way of carrying out religious rites and ceremonies that are to be used by the Church's minister in the celebration of the sacraments, blessings and devotions.

Rock The Aramaic word for rock is *kepha* and Jesus gives the name Kephas or Cephas to the Apostle Simon because he is the rock on which the Church is built (Matthew 16:18). In Greek the word for rock is *petra* from which the name Peter comes. This is a pun on the name and emphasises Simon Peter's special role in the early Church.

Roman rite The official liturgy of the Roman Catholic Church.

Rome The capital of the ancient Roman Empire. The Romans under Pompey invaded Palestine in 63 BCE and governed it as an occupied territory. Roman rule over the whole Mediterranean area in the first century CE made it possible for Christianity to spread. Often called 'the Eternal City', Rome became the centre of the Christian movement and has always been the first city of Roman Catholicism.

Rosary The name given to the devotion (and the object used) of meditating on the events in the life of Jesus Christ as seen through Mary's eyes in the Joyful, Sorrowful and Glorious mysteries. Groups of beads on a chain or string assist in praying the ten Hail Marys, the Our Father and the Glory Be for each of the fifteen decades. The rosary's origin is uncertain, but it was promoted by the order of Dominicans and has been a popular form of prayer for over five hundred years.

Rosary

Rubrics (Latin *rubrica,* red earth for colouring.) The rules of Church ceremonies that explain what actions are to be performed and what prayers are to be said. They are printed in the liturgical books in red.

Russian Church The national Church of Russia (before 1918) made up mostly of Russian Orthodox Christians of the Byzantine rite.

Sabbath (Hebrew *shabbat,* stop or cease.) The seventh day of the week is a holy day in the Jewish religion and is marked by rest from work, and by prayer to God. Jews observe the Sabbath from sunset on Friday until sunset on Saturday. All the main Christian churches observe the Sabbath on Sunday in commemoration of the day on which Christ rose from the dead.

Sacrament (Latin *sacramentum,* a sacred thing.) A visible sign of God's invisible presence. The seven sacraments of the Church are signs of God's presence and celebrate in a special way the new life which Jesus brings us. This new life of the risen Christ is called grace and it helps us to grow closer to God and each other. The seven sacraments are: Baptism, Confirmation, Eucharist, Penance, Anointing of the Sick, Orders and Marriage.

Sacramental An object that is a sacred sign that grace is being given by God to anyone who uses the sacramental with faith and devotion. Examples of sacramentals are holy water, rosary beads, crucifixes, statues, candles.

Sacramentary Another name for the Roman Missal, which is a book containing the prayers for the different kinds of Masses that can be celebrated. The Sacramentary is the large book used by the priest at Mass.

Sacraments of initiation Baptism, Confirmation and Eucharist are the sacraments of initiation. These sacraments are received at a person's entry or initiation into the Church which is the Christian community.

Sacraments of the sick The sacraments of Reconciliation, Eucharist and the Anointing of the Sick are the sacraments celebrated with people who are sick at home or in hospital.

Sacred Something that is highly respected and set aside for a special purpose is said to be sacred, e.g. a church, a wedding ring. For Christians, Jesus Christ is a sacred person; their belief in God is sacred; the Christian way of life and its values are sacred. When Christians celebrate all these things, then the actions, songs, words and objects they use also become sacred. All human beings are sacred because they are created in God's image. All Christians are sacred because they are members of Christ.

Sacred Heart of Jesus This is a devotion in the Church which emphasises that the human heart of Jesus is a sign of his love for all people. The heart full of love was pierced with a spear. In pictures and statues Jesus is shown pointing to his heart, which is burning with love for all humanity. The feast of the Sacred Heart is celebrated on the Friday after Trinity Sunday.

Sacred mysteries The sacred mysteries are the liturgical actions which recall and celebrate the events of the salvation of the human race, that is, the life, death and resurrection of Jesus Christ, his return to the Father and his abiding presence among his people.

Sacrifice (Latin *sacrificare,* make sacred.) The offering of something to gods in order to please them. The Israelites offered a part of their crops or animals as an act of worship to God, to ask for favours and forgiveness of their sins, and as a sign of their special relationship or covenant with God. They saw sacrifice as a way of drawing close to God. Christ's death on the cross may be called a sacrifice because it sums up the Incarnation and Christ's whole life of obedience to God (Philippians 2:8). By dying on the cross Jesus Christ freely offered himself as an act of self-giving love that made up for the sins of all people (Ephesians 5:2). However, it was not a sacrifice in the pagan sense where a victim was killed as an act or worship to a god.

Sacrilege (Latin *sacrilegium*, the stealing of something sacred.) Insulting or irreverent behaviour, abuse of or violent action towards sacred persons or objects.

Sacristy The room in the church in which are kept the vestments, linens and other articles used at Mass and other celebrations and services.

Sadducees An upper-class, priestly group in Judaism, formed around 150 BCE. They opposed the Pharisees in some of their beliefs, e.g. they did not believe in the resurrection of the body. They took their name from Zadok, who was the great high priest during the reign of King Solomon. The Sadducees are mentioned in the gospels and some of them were more interested in political than religious ideas.

Saint (Latin *sanctus*, holy, sacred.) (1) A person who is devoted to serving God and other people. The Christians in New Testament times called each other saints because they regarded themselves as specially set aside from the pagan world and dedicated to God and Jesus Christ through Baptism. The Greek word *hagios* means separate, not in the bad sense of isolated, but in the sense of being related to God and therefore not open to bad use. All Christians are called by God to be holy in the way they devote themselves to the glory of God and the service of their neighbour. (2) A person who is in heaven. Sometimes the Church recognises the status of such a person officially by the process of canonisation. The Pope then canonises a saint.

Salvation (Latin *salus*, health; Greek *soteria*, safe return home.) Being saved from danger and enemies. In the Old Testament the Hebrews experienced salvation when they were delivered from slavery in Egypt. They believed that God would continue to save them from their enemies and would grant them complete salvation and happiness at the end of time. In the New Testament, Jesus is described as the one who saves the human race from the power of evil through his incarnation, life, death and resurrection. We are saved when we are fully united with God and one another.

Salvation Army A religious organisation founded in England by William Booth in 1865 to revive religion among ordinary working people. It is set up like a Christian army and its members hold different ranks and wear a special uniform. The Army has the same teaching as the Protestant evangelical churches and is famous for its charitable work among the poor and homeless.

Salvation history The people of Israel saw history as a period of time and events in which God was leading them to salvation. Christians also believe that history is directed by God who is leading people of good will toward the kingdom of God. Salvation history begins with creation and ends with the second coming of Christ. All history leads up to and flows from the central event of salvation history which is the life-saving activity of Jesus Christ.

Samaria Capital city of the northern kingdom of Israel, which fell to the Assyrians in 721 BCE. In the time of Jesus the district of Samaria was the province between Judea in the south, and Galilee in the far north.

Samaritans Inhabitants of Samaria. The Jews claim that the Samaritans intermarried with Assyrians and so are not truly Jewish. The Samaritans deny this and claim that their sacred mountain, Gerizim, not Jerusalem, is the true place of worship. Samaritans share some of their beliefs with Islam. In the time of Jesus, Jews and Samaritans disliked each other. Some Samaritans were among the first to believe in Jesus. Today there are a little over 500 Samaritans living in Israel and still observing their own form of the law of Moses, regarding the first five books of the Bible as the only scripture.

Sanctuary (Latin *sanctuarium*, a place for sacred things.) (1) A sacred or holy place. (2) In Church buildings it is that part of the church where the altar is.

Sanhedrin (Greek *synedrion*, sitting together, council.) The supreme council of the Jews, made up of seventy-one people: elders of the chief families, former high priests, and scribes. The sanhedrin is said to have begun with the seventy elders who advised Moses (Numbers 11:10–24) but it ceased to exist as a political body after the destruction of Jerusalem in 70 CE.

Satan (Hebrew *satan*, opponent.) In the Hebrew scriptures the satan is a mythical character who has the power to test human beings. In the time of Jesus Satan was called the prince of evil spirits. The first Christians thought of Satan as a spirit representing all the forces of evil. Satan is the one who always tries to break down the friendship between people and God. Lucifer is another name for Satan.

Saviour (Latin *salvator*, one who saves.) A title given to Jesus Christ because he saved the world from the power of evil by his life, death and resurrection.

Sayings of Jesus The followers of Jesus may well have had written collections of sayings that Jesus uttered during his life. These sayings would have strengthened their belief in the risen Jesus and guided them in their lives. Many New Testament scholars believe that stories about Jesus were added to these collections of sayings and that, by the end of the first century CE, were written as the four gospels that we possess today. *See also* Q.

Scapular (Latin *scapulae*, shoulders.) (1) Part of a religious habit consisting of a piece of cloth, shoulder wide, which slips over the head and hangs down, front and back, to a certain length. (2) A sacramental which is a small imitation of the larger form. It consists of two small pieces of cloth joined by strings and worn around the neck, hanging down front and back. Some people wear the scapular as a sign of devotion to the Most Blessed Virgin Mary.

Schism (Greek *schisma*, split.) A separation from, or a division within, a Church or religious body because of some differences in teachings. The separation of the Eastern churches from the Roman Church is called a schism. *See also* Great Schism.

Scribes Official writers of documents in ancient times, when few people could read and write. The Jewish scribes in the time of Jesus were highly educated interpreters and teachers of the law. They were leaders in the community and some of them were hostile to Jesus because he threatened their influence. Many of the scribes were Pharisees. The scribes were unpaid and had to obtain other employment to support themselves.

Scriptures Sacred writings of a religious group. The Christian Bible, which is made up of the Hebrew scriptures and the New Testament, is inspired by God, which means that it contains the truth that God wants us to know about for the sake of our salvation. *See* Bible.

Second coming A phrase used to refer to the future coming of Christ. The New Testament writers used the Greek word *parousia* to mean the second coming of Christ at the end of the world. Christians believe that Jesus Christ will come at the end of the world to judge both good and bad people and bring complete happiness to those who love God and have remained faithful to the message of the gospels.

Second Vatican Council The twenty-first ecumenical (universal) council, called by Pope John XXIII to give the Church an opportunity to a) examine its own life and activity in order to encourage spiritual renewal in the light of the Gospel, b) promote peace and the unity of all people and c) bring the Church up to date with modern thinking. Pope John opened the Council on 11 October 1962 and Pope Paul VI closed it in 1965. Sixteen official documents were written by this gathering of bishops. Four Constitutions, nine Decrees and three Declarations contain the teachings of this Council.

Sect (Latin *secta*, path, a following.) (1) A group of people who belong to a particular religious faith. (2) A group that has broken away from the main body of believers in a religion, e.g. Christianity began as a breakaway movement or sect of Judaism.

Sectarianism Strong devotion to a particular sect or religion. Very often this strong devotion can lead people to be unreasonable and unfair in their dislike of other religions.

Secular (Latin *saeculum*, a period of time, the times.) Things of the world that are not religious or sacred, e.g. sacred music is sung or played in church, while secular music is usually heard on the radio, and may not have anything to do with religious matters.

Secular clergy Priests who work 'in the world', that is, those priests who belong to a diocese and work under the authority of and in co-operation with the bishop of the diocese. They are often called diocesan clergy and their work is in the diocese, either in special works nominated by the bishop or most often in parishes of the diocese.

Secularism A view of life that excludes God and religious attitudes from human thinking and living.

Seder meal (Hebrew *seder*, order.) The Jewish ceremonial meal held on the first night of Passover. Various symbolic dishes are eaten and the whole dinner becomes a ceremony recalling how God cared for the Jewish people and rescued them from slavery in Egypt.

Seminary (Latin *seminarium*, seedbed.) A college in which those men who believe they are called to minister as priests are educated. These men are called seminarians.

Septuagint (Latin *septuaginta*, seventy.) Name given to the translation into Greek of the Hebrew scriptures, supposedly by seventy scholars, in the third century BCE. It was used by Jews who could not read Hebrew in countries where they spoke only Greek. This Greek translation of the scriptures was used by the early Greek-speaking Christians. The Septuagint is often referred to by the Latin numerals LXX.

Sermon on the mount A collection of the sayings of Jesus put together by Matthew in his gospel (chapters 5–7) and presented as a sermon. These sayings contain the teachings of Jesus and show what he expects of his followers.

Servant of the Lord The figure described in Isaiah 40–55. He is a charismatic leader who heals others through his innocent suffering and brings salvation through his death. In the New Testament Jesus is identified with this servant who carries out the will of God and saves his people through suffering (Acts 3:26).

Service (Latin *servitium*, slavery, subjection.) (1) The name given to a religious or paraliturgical ceremony. It is not normally used in referring to the Mass. (2) Any social or religious work that is done to help others.

Shalom Hebrew word meaning 'peace'. *See also* Peace *and* Sign of Peace.

Shekel An amount of money used by the ancient Israelites. A shekel was equal to four days' pay for a farm labourer.

Sheol Hebrew word meaning 'the abode of the dead'. The Israelites thought that Sheol was a place of darkness where the dead do nothing at all. Towards the time of Jesus they developed their understanding of Sheol and regarded it as a place for the wicked only, while the good people went to Paradise.

Shepherd A person who looks after sheep. The prophets criticised the bad rulers of Israel for being like bad shepherds who did not care about their sheep. They referred to God as the good shepherd who continually looked after the people of Israel. Jesus called himself the good shepherd who loves and watches over his followers.

Sign of peace In the Mass, just before Communion, the priest invites the people to share a sign of peace with each other. It is a sign of respect and friendship towards our fellow Christians, and reminds us that we cannot approach Holy Communion if we do not love our neighbour.

Sign of the cross A sacramental action imitating the shape of a cross by touching the forehead, breast and left and right shoulders with right hand (or right and left shoulders with three fingers of the right hand, in Eastern Catholic rites). While doing this action, we say or think to ourselves the words: 'In the name of the Father, and of the Son, and of the Holy Spirit. Amen.'

Sikh A Hindi word meaning 'disciple'. A Sikh is a member of a religious sect founded in the sixteenth century in north-western India by a Hindu reformer.

Sin (Latin *sons*, hurtful, guilty.) Hebrew words for sin mean to shoot an arrow and 'miss the mark', i.e. to fail to achieve a goal. To sin is to be deliberately unfaithful to what God asks of us. In the New Testament, sin is the result of failing to live the new life in Christ. This failure affects our relationship with God, other people and ourselves.

Sister The title of a woman who is a member of a religious order or congregation.

Slavery It was common for rich people in ancient times to have slaves working for them. Slaves were generally foreigners and prisoners of war who were bought and sold in the marketplace. Sometimes a person who was too poor to pay for food would sell himself and his family as slaves. The Israelites had laws that provided for the release of slaves under certain conditions. Some of the wealthier Christians of the first century also had slaves in their households. The first Christians saw the life, death and resurrection of Jesus as something that released them from the slavery of sin and the power of evil.

Social action Social action takes place when people show fairness and love in their dealings with each other. Christian social action is based on the words of Jesus, that whatever we do to each other we do to Jesus himself (Matthew 25:40).

Social justice Social justice means that everybody, including governments, organisations and individuals, should treat all other people with dignity according to their rights as human beings. True social justice does not allow the existence of favouritism, racism or any discrimination against other people. The Church has always been concerned for social justice in its teaching.

Sodality (Latin *sodalitus*, society.) A group or society within the parish whose members pray together and often do good works to help others.

Son of God In the Hebrew scriptures the kings of Israel were called sons of God because they were specially chosen by God to lead the people of Israel. The early Christians reflected on the resurrection of Jesus and came to believe in his unique character and applied to him the title Son of God. This title describes a far more intimate union with God than the one that existed between God and the kings of Israel. Jesus is the only Son of God, and is both God and man.

Son of man This name first appears in the Book of Daniel (chapter 7) to describe a figure that symbolises the true people of God who will be given everlasting power and glory. In the New Testament Jesus is called the son of man, who, like the son of man in the Book of Daniel, would be given honour and power and would set up an everlasting kingdom. The title son of man is used in the New Testament to describe Jesus as the Messiah.

Soul The life spirit of a person; the spark of life that makes me ME. The Hebrews did not consider the soul to be separate from the body, as the Greeks did. New Testament writers speak of the 'spirit' as the life-giving force of a person.

Speaking in tongues *See* Tongues.

Spirit (Latin *spiritus*, breathing.) The thing that gives life to a person. The Spirit of God was understood by the Hebrews to be a force giving life and goodness to humans. It is a free gift from God. Supernatural beings, who do not have physical bodies, are called spirits. *See also* Holy Spirit.

Spirituality Human beings are made up of body and spirit. To be spiritual means to live in the presence of God according to the values of the spirit. Spirituality is concerned with the way people live in relationship with God. For Christians this means living the Christian life of faith in God, of hope in God's goodness and mercy, and of love for God, other people and the world around us.

Sponsor (1) The person who speaks for one in baptism and has some responsibility for helping the baptised person spiritually. *See also* Godparent. (2) One who takes care that the person confirmed tries to live the Christian life well. The sponsor must be a person who has already been confirmed. The Church considers it desirable the same person be sponsor for baptism and confirmation.

Stations of the cross Also called 'the way of the cross', this devotion consists of prayers and meditations on the sufferings of Jesus as he carried his cross to Calvary and was crucified. Pictures or representations of the fourteen (sometimes more) stations are usually around the walls of the church, and the leader moves from one to the next reciting prayers. The people respond to these prayers and spend time thinking about the sufferings of Jesus. The stations may also be carried our privately and individually.

Steward An official, in New Testament times, who directed the affairs of a large household. He supervised the servants and looked after the buying of food, wine, kitchen supplies, etc. Jesus says that his followers must be like stewards who take great care to nourish their spiritual life as Christians. Like stewards, all people will have to give an account of their lives.

Stigmata (Greek *stigmata*, marks, tattoos.) These are the marks of the wounds on the body of Jesus as he was crucified. Some men and women have had these marks on their bodies and have endured great pain as a result. The stigmata have been regarded as a sign of holiness and special favour given to a person. There are about three hundred recorded cases and Padre Pio of Italy was probably the best known modern stigmatist.

Stipend (Latin *stipendium*, contribution.) (1) A contribution or offering that people make to a priest when they ask him to celebrate a Mass for a special intention, e.g. for a deceased relative, for a wedding. It is not payment for a Mass but shows that the people are concerned for the support of the Church's ordained minister. (2) A living allowance that enables members of religious congregations or other appointed persons to carry our their ministry.

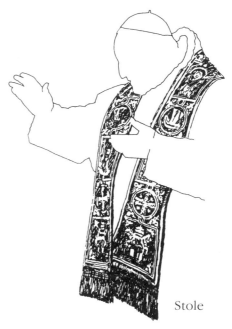

Stole

Stole (Latin *stola*, a long gown.) A vestment that now consists of a long, narrow strip of cloth, matching in colour the vestments of the feast or season, and worn by bishops, priests and deacons as a sign of their official ministry of the sacraments and in preaching. It goes around the neck with both ends hanging down the front.

Stoning In Israelite society, people who committed certain serious crimes (e.g. worshipping another god, blasphemy, adultery) could be punished by being stoned. The victim was stripped, knocked down on the scaffold and then pelted with stones by the community. This meant that the judgement and punishment were shared, and no single person struck the fatal blow.

Succoth (Hebrew *succah*, hut, tent.) The feast of tents or tabernacles was one of Israel's three great festivals. It was celebrated in autumn, at the end of the agricultural year. It recalls the time when the Israelites wandered through the desert after they left Egypt and put up tents wherever they stopped to camp. Today, Jews keep the feast by building, in their yard or on the verandah, small huts out of branches. They spend a little time in the hut during each of the seven days of the festival season.

Suffering Pain or distress. The Israelites thought suffering was brought about by evil. Biblical writers tried to explain why good people suffer and came to the conclusion that suffering led people away from themselves and towards God, or that people would be freed from their guilt if they underwent suffering. The suffering of Jesus takes away the sins of the world because he freely laid down his life so that others might live. Christians who suffer believe that, in some mysterious way, they share in what Christ went through on the cross.

Suffering servant The idea of the suffering servant comes from the songs of the Servant of Yahweh recorded in Isaiah (42:1–4; 50:4–11; 52:13; 53:12). *See* Servant of the Lord.

Suicide (Latin *sui*, self; *cidium*, killing.) When a person deliberately takes their own life they commit suicide. Although the Church has always regarded suicide as wrong, because it goes against God's sacred gift of life and human dignity, it realises that most people only commit suicide when they are extremely troubled or desperate. Consequently, these people may not be fully responsible for what they do.

Summa Theologiae The summary of theology. This is an enormous work written by St Thomas Aquinas between 1266 and 1273. Thomas died before he could finish his Summa. It contains an organised summary of sacred knowledge and has been one of the most influential reference books of Catholic knowledge.

Sunday Early Christians met together to celebrate the Eucharist on Sunday, the first day of the week, because it was the day of Christ's resurrection. Every Sunday then is a weekly celebration of Easter, so it is a day of hope and joy in the resurrection of Jesus Christ. In today's church, Catholics still meet on Sunday to celebrate the Eucharist. Saturday evening celebrations also take place in accordance with the old custom that the day extends from sunset to sunset. It is important for the faith and spiritual life of Christians that they give some time every week to community worship.

Syllabus of Errors A list of eighty 'errors' of nineteenth-century learning and thinking that were condemned by Pope Pius IX in 1864.

Symbol (Greek *symballein*, bring together [things or ideas].) The term given to something that is usually visible and reminds us of something else that is invisible but connected with it. For example, a national flag is the symbol of a country and the unity of its loyal citizens. Symbols stimulate our minds and help us gain a greater understanding of the presence of God that lies behind the symbol. For instance, when Jesus Christ is called the Word of God it means that his person and his whole life are a symbol of what God wants to tell us about God and God's plan for us. The creeds are also called symbols of faith because they bring together dogmatic statements that are summary expressions of basic Christian truths.

Synagogue (Greek *synagein*, gather together.) A Jewish place of assembly for prayer and instruction. It is a meeting house where the Jewish community prays and studies the law. The synagogue came into existence in places that were far away from the Temple in Jerusalem. In these areas Temple worship was impossible, so the synagogue became a substitute place of prayer and community meeting. From ancient times, Jews outside of Jerusalem have assembled each Sabbath in synagogues to pray and read the scriptures.

Synod (Greek *synodos*, assembly.) An official meeting in a diocese of clergy and other appointed representatives called to discuss areas of concern in the Church's life.

Synod of bishops The gathering of bishops on an international, national or regional level to discuss areas of concern in the Church's life. The name applies particularly to the international gathering of bishops that is held in Rome from time to time, in order to assist the Pope in matters concerning the whole Church.

Synoptic Gospels (Greek *synopsis*, a seeing all together.) The gospels of Matthew, Mark and Luke are called the synoptic gospels because when they are read side by side it is clear that they share certain common elements. These three gospels have so much material in common that it is believed that Matthew and Luke borrowed stories and sayings about Jesus from Mark, which is the oldest of the three.

Syrian rite The rite for the liturgy and ceremonies used by Catholic Syrians, Malankarese and the Orthodox Jacobites of Syria and Malabar. It is sometimes called the liturgy of St James.

Tabernacle (Latin *tabernaculum*, little hut, booth.) (1) The tent used by the Jews as a portable place of worship as they wandered through the desert before arriving at the Promised Land. (2) A fixed, suitably adorned and solid place in a church where the Blessed Sacrament is kept.

Taizé A monastery in France that is a centre of prayer and pilgrimage for Christians of all denominations.

Taizé chant A style of singing one simple phrase over and over again in a very prayerful and thoughtful way. This style of singing is popular at Taizé.

Talent Sum of money used in New Testament times. It is about $480. From the story in Matthew 25:14–30 comes the idea that a talent is a gift or quality received from God.

Talmud An Aramaic word meaning 'teaching'. It is a kind of encyclopedia of Jewish law and the central document of Jewish literature, second to the Hebrew Scriptures. It was written in stages between the second and sixth centuries CE.

Taoism A way of life and a religion said to have been founded by Lao-tzu in China in the fifth century BCE. Taoism (pronounced: dowism) teaches that one should not interfere with the course of nature, but that everything in the world is designed to exist in harmony. Sincerity and honesty are among the chief characteristics of a good Taoist. The Tao Te Ching is the sacred writing of Taoism.

Taxes Money paid to a government for the running of a country. In New Testament times the Jews hated paying money to Rome, because it was an admission that they had been conquered by a foreign power.

Temple A building where people worship a god or gods. However, the magnificent Temple of Solomon in Jerusalem was more than just a place of worship. It was the sign of God's presence among the chosen people. The poets of Israel expressed the love of the people for their Temple in the Psalms, e.g. 83, 121. The most sacred part of the building was a room divided in two by a veil. The larger half was the 'Holy' and the other part was the 'Holy of Holies'. The first Temple in Jerusalem was built by King Solomon around 931 BCE and was destroyed by the Babylonians in 587 BCE. The second Temple was completed around 515 BCE. It was renovated by King Herod the Great and finally destroyed by the Romans in 70 CE. In the New Testament Jesus is called the new Temple because where he is there God is present.

Ten Commandments Laws given to the Israelite people by Moses (Exodus 20). They were part of the covenant between God and Israel. In order to remain faithful to the covenant, the people of Israel were obliged to keep the Ten Commandments along with many other laws.

Testament (Latin *testamentum*, a will.) It came to mean an arrangement or covenant between people. The Hebrew scriptures and the whole Jewish tradition are centred on the covenant that God made with Israel through Moses, while the New Testament is centred on the new covenant of Jesus Christ. The scriptures or sacred writings of both testaments are inspired by God and contain truths that God has revealed to us.

Theology (Greek *theologia*, science of things related to God.) The ordered study of God, the qualities of God, God's relations with the created universe, and religious truths. Theology is usually undertaken by believers who are seeking understanding.

Thurible *See* Censer.

Tongues   Speaking in tongues was considered by early Christians to be a gift from the Holy Spirit. The believer at prayer uttered jumbled words and sounds that other people could not understand. These utterances were expressions that arose from the heart without being restricted by careful thinking. Today, praying in tongues occurs particularly at charismatic prayer meetings.

Torah   Hebrew word for 'guidance', 'way'. It came to refer to the law of Israel as a guide for living a good life as a Jew. It also includes the Pentateuch, i.e. the first five books of the Bible. Torah is sacred to the Jews and contains revelation from God.

Torah

Tradition   (Latin *traditio*, handing down.) Tradition is the process by which the faith is handed on and it is also that which is handed on. This includes the scriptures, the teachings of the Church, the writings of the Fathers, the liturgical practices of the Church and the living faith of the Church throughout the ages.

Transfiguration   An event in the life of Jesus when his appearance became radiant in the presence of three disciples on a mountaintop (Matthew 17:1–9; Mark 9:2–10; Luke 9:28–36). The episode reveals to us that Jesus is the Son of God who is glorified by the Father.

Trent, Council of (1545–1563)   The nineteenth ecumenical council was held in the Italian city of Trent. It was the Roman Catholic response to Luther and the Protestant Reformation. The Council drew up documents that contained Church teaching on scripture, original sin, grace, the seven sacraments etc., and insisted on an improved training program for priests. The teachings of this council were the main guidelines for Catholic life until the Second Vatican Council.

Tribune   Officer in the Roman army commanding a cohort, i.e. between 600 and 1000 men.

Tridentine Mass   Mass celebrated in Latin according to the ritual laid down by the Council of Trent. This form was replaced by the new formula of the Second Vatican Council which insisted that the rites for Mass be simplified, that the Mass be celebrated in the language of the people, and that the faithful be given the opportunity to take their proper part. Special permission now has to be granted by the bishop before a priest can celebrate the Tridentine Mass.

Triduum   (Latin *triduum*, three days.) A three-day period of prayer. *See also* Easter Triduum.

Trinity   One of the principal doctrines of the Catholic faith which expresses belief in one God as three distinct persons: Father, Son and Holy Spirit. This is a great mystery of the Christian faith and cannot be fully explained in human language.

Ukrainian rite The Byzantine rite used in the liturgies of both Orthodox and Catholic Christians in the Ukraine, Byelorussia, Hungary, Romania, Slovenia and Yugoslavia, and by those who emigrated from those lands to other countries. It is conducted in the Old Slavonic, Romanian and Ukrainian languages.

Ultramontanism Meaning 'beyond the mountains, the Alps'. It is a form of rigid thinking that looks 'beyond the mountains' to the Pope in Rome rather than to the local Church for guidance. The Ultramontanes wanted all Church authority to be centralised in Rome because they believed that only a strong papacy could protect the Church against errors and unacceptable practices.

Uniate (Uniat) churches Eastern churches that are organised under the direction of their own Patriarchs who are in communion with the Pope. They have their own liturgy, rites and laws but are different from the Eastern Orthodox churches, which are still separated from Rome as a result of the east-west Schism of 1054. The Uniate churches belong to the Chaldean, Syrian, Maronite, Coptic, Armenian and Byzantine rites.

Uniting Church An Australian Church formed in 1977 from the union of the Congregational, Methodist and some Presbyterian churches. The Uniting Church has placed strong emphasis on its identity as an Australian church. It has also taken a strong stand on social issues such as Aboriginal land rights, poverty and nuclear disarmament.

Unleavened bread Bread or cakes baked without yeast and used by the Jews as food, especially at certain feasts, e.g. Passover. In the Roman Catholic Church the bread of the Eucharist is traditionally unleavened, while the Eastern churches use leavened bread.

Vatican (Latin *collis vaticanus* is the name of a hill in Rome.) It is the shortened form of the name of the Vatican City, which is an independent state ruled over by the Pope. The central administration of the Catholic Church is located in the Vatican.

Vatican Council A meeting in the Vatican (St Peter's Basilica) of all the bishops of the Catholic Church.

Vatican Council I The twentieth ecumenical council, called by Pope Pius IX and held in the Vatican from December 1869 to October 1870. The aim of this council was to look for a remedy for the evils that were seen in the Church and society at the time. This council is best known for the decree that declared the infallibility of the Pope when he spoke on matters of faith and morals. *See also* Infallibility.

Vatican II *See* Second Vatican Council.

Vernacular (Latin *vernaculus*, native.) The native language of a particular people or place. The liturgy of the Roman rite is now celebrated in the vernacular as well as in Latin.

Vespers (Latin *vespera*, evening.) (1) A religious service celebrated in the afternoon. (2) Part of the Divine Office recited in the afternoon or evening.

Vestments Garments worn by bishops, priests, deacons and assistants at liturgical ceremonies. They are based on the style of clothes worn by people in the early days of Christianity. Today they are worn as part of the continuing traditional practice of the church, a sign that the wearer has a special part to play in the liturgy and as a way of adding solemnity to the occasion.

Viaticum (Latin *viaticum*, food for a journey.) Holy Communion given to a person who is dying.

Vicar (Latin *vicarius*, substitute, representative.) (1) The Pope as the representative on earth of Christ. (2) A clergyman who represents the Pope or a bishop. (3) An Anglican clergyman who acts as the priest of a parish.

Vicar-General A priest appointed by the bishop to assist him in governing the diocese.

Vigil (Latin *vigilia*, watch.) (1) People take part in a vigil when they spend all or part of the night in praying or taking part in devotional activities. (2) The eve or night before a Church festival, e.g. Holy Saturday is the vigil of Easter.

Vincent de Paul, Society of An international society of Catholic lay people who serve as volunteers and perform works of charity for the poor. Antoine Frederic Ozanam (1813–53), together with some other young men, founded the Society in Paris in 1833.

Virgin (Latin *virgo*, young girl.) A person, male or female, who has had no sexual relations with any other person. In the Catholic tradition virginity is important as part of dedicating oneself in a special way to God and the service of others through some form of ministry.

Virgin birth The belief that Jesus became a human being without the co-operation of a human father. This belief is based on the events recorded in Matthew 1:18–25 and Luke 2:1–2, as well as the teaching of the Church.

Virgin Mary Mary, the wife of Joseph of Nazareth and the mother of Jesus. She does not figure largely in the New Testament, but Christians have always honoured Mary as the virgin mother of the redeemer. They have cultivated a strong devotion to Mary because of her part in God's plan for the salvation of the human race.

Virtue (Latin *virtus*, excellence, strength.) A quality of doing moral good. For example, kindness is a virtue. The virtues of faith, hope and charity are called the theological virtues because they are given by God. *See also* Cardinal virtues.

Vocation (Latin *vocatio*, a calling.) A calling to follow a particular career or occupation in life. Because they belong to Christ through baptism, all Christians have a vocation to become mature disciples of Christ and to become holy as active members of the Church community. They help spread the kingdom of God through a special Christian vocation as lay persons, consecrated religious, or ordained ministers.

Votive Mass A Mass celebrated for a particular intention or devotion of the priest or people, e.g. Votive Mass of the Holy Spirit at the start of the school year.

Vow A voluntary and deliberate promise made to God to do something that is good and possible. A vow may be made privately or publicly. It is public if it is accepted officially and in front of witnesses in the name of the church, e.g. vows of poverty, chastity and obedience, taken by members of religious orders, are sometimes called the Evangelical Counsels.

Vulgate (Latin *vulgus*, the common people.) Translation of the Bible, made by St Jerome, from the original Hebrew and Greek languages into the Latin language of the common people of his time. St Jerome wrote his translation between 383 and 405 CE.

Way The first Christians called themselves followers of 'the way' (Acts 9:2; 19:9,23). Christianity is a way of life; living according to 'the way of the Lord'.

Way of the cross *See* Stations of the cross.

Widow A woman whose husband has died. The first Christians were careful to look after widows and orphans who had nobody to provide for them (Acts 6:1).

Wisdom The quality of being wise and knowing what is right. The wisdom books in the Bible contain wise sayings and stories about wise people. These books are Proverbs, Ecclesiastes, Job, The Wisdom of Solomon and Sirach (Ecclesiasticus).

Witness (Greek *martus*, witness, martyr.) A person who is present and sees an event take place. Someone who declares some truth about God and Jesus. When we live good lives as Christians we give witness to others of our faith.

Word of God The will of God is made known to humans through the spoken word. The prophets spoke out on behalf of God and so they spoke the word of God. The Hebrew word *davar* means 'word, news, action, thing, history, concern', so when we say the Bible is the word of God it means a lot more than just the spoken or written word. It means the story of God and the whole activity of God in favour of the chosen people. The word of God is effective because what God says actually takes place (Genesis 1). Jesus is called the Word of God in the fourth gospel because he reveals to us what we need to know about God.

Women in the Church Pope John XXIII drew attention to the dignity of women in the Church and since Vatican II many Catholic women have asked why there are restrictions on women's participation in the life of the Church. Pope John Paul II emphasised the dignity of women in his apostolic letter *Mulieris Dignitatem* but he did not deal with many of the important questions, concerning some traditions of the male-dominated Church, that women are asking today.

Works of mercy Acts of charity performed with the intention of helping another person spiritually and/or physically (Matthew 25:31–46). The spiritual works of mercy are: reminding people of their duty if we see them going astray; teaching, especially the truths of faith; consoling those who are in sorrow; being patient with others; forgiving those who injure us; praying for the living and the dead. The corporal or physical works of mercy are: feeding the hungry; giving drink to the thirsty; giving clothes to the poor; helping those in prison; giving shelter to the homeless; visiting the sick; burying the dead.

World Council of Churches Established 23 August 1948 in Amsterdam, it is an international, ecumenical body of Churches that consult with one another and co-operate in matters of Church teaching, worship, missionary work and other matters of concern. The Catholic Church is not a member, but a permanent representative for the Vatican attends meetings as an observer.

Worship Worship occurs when humans turn to God in appreciation of the goodness and grandeur of God. The official public worship of the Church is the liturgy for which the people gather to remember and celebrate all that God has done for them.

Yahweh Hebrew name for God. It means 'the one who brings everything into being'. It describes God as creator and life itself. The name was so sacred it was spoken only once a year by the High Priest. When speaking of God, the Israelites generally used the expression 'Adonai', which means 'my Lord'. Jews today follow the same practice.

Your Eminence A form of address used when speaking to a cardinal.

Your Grace A form of address used when speaking to an archbishop.

Your Holiness A form of address used when speaking to the Pope.

Zealot (Greek *zelotes*, one who is enthusiastic, a fanatic.) The Zealots were Jews who were strict about the keeping of the law. In the time of Jesus they were opposed to the Romans and longed for the coming of the Messiah who would crush the enemy power. The Zealots wanted to overthrow the Romans by violent means and set up a free Jewish state. They used the same tactics against the Romans as modern political terrorists. One of the apostles of Jesus had been a Zealot and he was called Simon the Zealot.

Zen A form of Buddhism from China that was further developed in Japan. Zen claims a person can know truth directly through inner experience. Meditation and contemplation are the key practices for Zen followers.

Zion (1) The Hebrew name for the hill on which the Temple of Jerusalem was built. It has come to mean the city of David; that is, Jerusalem itself. In Hebrew poetry, Jerusalem is sometimes called the daughter of Zion. (2) Today, Zion is another name for Israel as the national home of the Jews. (3) Another name for heaven, the final gathering place of all true believers.

Zionism A worldwide movement within Judaism that encourages Jews to return to the land of Israel in order to establish a homeland there. Some members of Orthodox Judaism oppose Zionism because they believe only God can re-establish the land of Israel through the activity of the Messiah.

Bible Characters

Aaron Elder brother of Moses and chief priest of the Israelites.

Abel Second son of Adam and Eve, who was killed by his envious brother, Cain.

Abraham The first of the patriarchs of Israel and father of the nation. He was known for his faithfulness to God.

Absalom Third son of King David. He and his followers rebelled against his father and were defeated in battle by David's army.

Ahasuerus Commonly known as Xerxes, king of Persia. He married the Jewish girl Esther.

Amos Eighth-century shepherd and prophet in Israel. He criticised the leaders of the people for giving up the worship of God and mistreating the poor.

Ananias A disciple in Damascus who gave Paul back his sight in the story of Acts 9.

Andrew Fisherman of Bethsaida who was among the first to follow Jesus. He was the brother of Simon Peter. He is the patron saint of Scotland.

Annas High priest in Jerusalem during the life of Jesus.

Antipas Also called Herod Antipas, son of Herod the Great. He was criticised by John the Baptist for unlawfully marrying his sister-in-law. Antipas ordered the beheading of John.

Barabbas A man who had been arrested for rebellion and murder. At the trial of Jesus the people obtained from Pontius Pilate the release of Barabbas and the condemnation of Jesus.

Barnabas A Levite from Cyprus who helped Paul spread the message of Christianity to the Gentiles. He was based in Antioch and introduced Paul to the Church there.

Bartholomew One of the twelve apostles. In John's gospel he is called Nathanael.

Bathsheba Wife of Uriah the Hittite and later of King David. She was the mother of King Solomon.

Benjamin Youngest of the twelve sons of Jacob and patriarch of one of the tribes of Israel.

Cain Mentioned in Genesis as the first son of Adam and Eve. He killed his brother Abel and was cursed by God. He was also protected by God.

Caiaphas High priest in Jerusalem 18–36 CE. Jesus was brought in trial before him.

Cleopas One of the disciples who met the risen Jesus along the way to Emmaus.

Daniel A hero of the Jewish people who lived during the time of the Exile in Babylon. He explained the dreams of King Nebuchadnezzar and was thrown into a den of lions for praying to God. However, the lions did not touch him.

David The second king of Israel and one of the most famous characters in Jewish history. He was a warrior king and a clever ruler who united all the tribes of Israel. In the first book of Samuel a story tells how David as a boy killed Goliath by knocking him out with a stone and cutting off his head.

Delilah A Philistine woman and wife of the strong man Samson. She tricked him and cut off his hair to take away his strength.

Elijah A ninth-century prophet of the northern kingdom of Israel who spoke against the worship of other gods.

Elisha A prophet and disciple of Elijah. He cured Naaman the Assyrian of leprosy.

Elizabeth Mentioned in Luke's Gospel as the wife of Zechariah and mother of John the Baptist. Mary the mother of Jesus visited Elizabeth when she heard that she was going to have a baby.

Esau Son of Isaac and Rebecca and twin brother of Jacob. He hated Jacob for tricking him out of his inheritance and wanted to kill him.

Esther A Jewish woman and wife of Ahasuerus, king of Persia. She is famous for having saved her people by asking the king to stop his chief minister, Haman, from killing the Jews in Persia.

Ezekiel A prophet of Judah during the Exile in Babylon. His prophecies are filled with descriptions of strange dreams and visions.

Gamaliel A respected Pharisee who spoke against the way some of the Jews were treating the first followers of Jesus.

Gideon One of the Judges of Israel. He led his men to victory against the Midianites.

Goliath A huge man who was a champion warrior of the Philistines. The second book of Samuel tells how he was killed by David.

Herod the Great King of Judea 40–4 BCE. He renovated the Temple in Jerusalem and made friends with the Romans. Matthew's Gospel has the story of how he tried to kill the baby Jesus.

Hosea Eighth-century prophet in northern Israel who tried to turn the people back to the worship of the one true God.

Isaac Son of Abraham and Sarah. He was almost sacrificed by his father as part of a test of Abraham's faith in God.

Israel A name that was given to Jacob and later became the name of the Jewish people.

Jacob Son of Isaac and Rebecca. He tricked his twin brother, Esau, out his inheritance. His twelve sons became the leaders of the twelve tribes of Israel.

James Son of Zebedee and one of the twelve apostles. Also called James the Great, or James the Elder.

Jeremiah Seventh-century prophet in Judah during the time of the Exile. He was unpopular because he criticised the bad behaviour of many of his fellow citizens.

Jesse Father of David, said to be an ancestor of Jesus.

Jezebel Pagan wife of King Ahab of Israel. She is described as a cunning and evil woman.

Job The main character of the Book of Job, which is a parable about a man who suffers a lot but still remains faithful to God.

John the Baptist A prophet in Judea who preached the coming of the Messiah. He washed or baptised people as a sign of cleansing and repentance.

John Son of Zebedee and one of the twelve apostles.

Jonah The main character in the Book of Jonah, which is a story about a prophet who was unwilling to do what God wanted of him. He later realised that he could not run away from God.

Jonathan Son of King Saul and special friend of David.

Joseph One of the sons of Jacob and Rachel. He was sold by his brothers as a slave and later became the Pharaoh's chief minister.

Joshua Leader of the Israelites after the death of Moses. He led the people into the Promised Land.

Judah The name of one of Jacob's twelve sons, of a tribe of Israel, and of the southern kingdom, which had Jerusalem as its capital.

Judas Iscariot An apostle who betrayed Jesus to the priests.

Judas Maccabaeus Jewish leader of a revolt against the Greek occupation of Palestine in the second century BCE.

Judith A woman of Judah who saved her people by cutting off the head of the Babylonian general Holofernes while he was asleep.

Lazarus Brother of Martha and Mary. John's gospel tells how Lazarus was raised from the dead by Jesus.

Luke Author of one of the gospels and the Acts of the Apostles.

Mark Author of the oldest of the four gospels.

Mary Mother of Jesus and wife of Joseph.

Mary of Bethany Sister of Martha and Lazarus. All three were close friends of Jesus.

Mary Magdalene Follower of Jesus who was with him at the crucifixion.

Matthew One of the twelve apostles, also called Levi, son of Alphaeus. Probably not the Matthew who wrote one of the gospels.

Moses Called by God to lead the people of Israel out of Egypt, he gave the people the law that he received from God on Mount Sinai.

Nicodemus A Pharisee who came to Jesus by night to learn about the kingdom of God. He helped bury Jesus' body after the crucifixion.

Noah A good man who, along with his family, was preserved from the punishment of the flood when God told him to build an ark.

Paul Outstanding preacher of the Gospel to the non-Jewish people of Asia Minor and Greece in the first century. Some of the letters he wrote to his communities are now part of the New Testament.

Peter Simon Peter, apostle and one of the early leaders of the church.

Philip One of the twelve apostles.

Pilate Pontius Pilate was the Roman Governor in Judea in the time of Jesus.

Rachel Wife of Jacob and mother of Joseph and Benjamin.

Rebecca Wife of Isaac and mother of Esau and Jacob.

Ruth Great-grandmother of King David. Her story is told in the Book of Ruth.

Salome Stepdaughter of Herod Antipas, who was pleased with her dancing and offered her whatever present she wanted. She asked for the head of John the Baptist.

Samson A Judge of Israel known for his great strength. He married a Philistine woman, Delilah, who betrayed him to her own people.

Samuel Prophet and last of the Judges of Israel. He anointed Saul and David as kings.

Saul First king of Israel.

Solomon Son of King David and king of Israel in the tenth century BCE. He built Israel into a powerful kingdom and was noted for his wisdom.

Stephen The first of the followers of Jesus to be killed for preaching the divinity and resurrection of Jesus.

Thomas One of the twelve apostles who is mentioned in John's gospel as refusing to believe in the resurrection of Jesus until he could see and touch Jesus for himself.

Zaccheus A rich tax collector of Jericho who climbed a tree to get a better view of Jesus. He was sorry for having been dishonest and was forgiven when Jesus came to his house.

Zechariah Prophet in Jerusalem in the late sixth century BCE when the people had returned from exile in Babylon.

Zachary Luke's Gospel contains the story of Zachary (also called Zacharias) and his wife Elizabeth, who were the parents of John the Baptist.

The Books of the First Testament

Pentateuch	The Historical Books	The Wisdom Books	The Prophetic Books
Genesis	Joshua	Job	Isaiah
Exodus	Judges	Psalms	Jeremiah
Leviticus	Ruth	Proverbs	Lamentations
Numbers	1 Samuel	Ecclesiastes	Baruch
Deuteronomy	2 Samuel	Song of Songs	Ezekiel
	1 Kings	Wisdom	Daniel
	2 Kings	Sirach	Hosea
	1 Chronicles		Joel
	2 Chronicles		Amos
	Ezra		Obadiah
	Nehemiah		Jonah
	Tobit		Micah
	Judith		Nahum
	Esther		Habakkuk
	1 Maccabees		Zephaniah
	2 Maccabees		Haggai
			Zechariah
			Malachi

The Books of the New Testament

The Gospels

Matthew

Mark

Luke

John

The Acts of the Apostles

The Letters

Romans	Titus
1 Corinthians	Philemon
2 Corinthians	Hebrews
Galatians	James
Ephesians	1 Peter
Philippians	2 Peter
Colossians	1 John
1 Thessalonians	2 John
2 Thessalonians	3 John
1 Timothy	Jude
2 Timothy	**Revelation**